BRIGHT NOTES

BABBITT
BY
SINCLAIR
LEWIS

Intelligent Education

D1525230

INFLUENCE PUBLISHERS

Nashville, Tennessee

BRIGHT NOTES: Babbitt

www.BrightNotes.com

ISBN: 978-1-645423-94-2 (Paperback)
ISBN: 978-1-645423-95-9 (eBook)

Published in accordance with the U.S. Copyright Office Orphan Works and Mass Digitization report of the register of copyrights, June 2015.

Originally published by Monarch Press.
Edward R. Winans, 1965
2019 Edition published by Influence Publishers.

Interior design by Lapiz Digital Services. Cover Design by Thinkpen Designs.

Printed in the United States of America.

Library of Congress Cataloging-in-Publication Data forthcoming.
Names: Intelligent Education
Title: BRIGHT NOTES: Babbitt
Subject: STU004000 STUDY AIDS / Book Notes

CONTENTS

1)   Introduction to Sinclair Lewis   1

2)   Textual Analysis
     Chapters 1–6   17
     Chapters 7–12   28
     Chapters 13–18   35
     Chapters 19–24   42
     Chapter 25–34   46

3)   Character Analyses   54

4)   General Commentary   67

5)   Critical Commentary   81

6)   Essay Questions and Answers for Review   86

7)   Bibliography and Guide to Research   94

INTRODUCTION TO SINCLAIR LEWIS

· ·

Harry Sinclair Lewis (1885–1951), the youngest of three sons of a country doctor, was born in Sauk Centre, Minnesota, on February 7, 1885. Although he was early interested in medicine, he did not, like his two brothers, follow in his father's footsteps. It was, however, the interests and experiences of these early years which provided much of the material for his novel on the medical profession, Arrowsmith, in 1925.

EARLY YEARS

During his early years Lewis received such rudimentary education as was possible in a town still largely crude and undeveloped, an education which he supplemented by a voracious if undirected reading. Never fully able to communicate with his father, whom he greatly admired, Lewis developed into a shy, sensitive, intellectually curious boy. Nor did the death of his mother when he was six and the rapid remarriage of his father do anything to bring about a greater understanding between father and son. Thus, left largely to himself and to the ministrations of a stepmother whom he learned to love, it is not surprising that he found Sauk Centre stifling.

EDUCATION

At seventeen, after a year at preparatory school, Lewis left Sauk Centre to study at Yale. Still awkward, gangly and socially inept, he found life at Yale no more congenial than it had been at Sauk Centre. Nor indeed was he ever able to enjoy the easy companionship of his contemporaries. Always self-conscious about his appearance (red-haired, gangly, and later scarred as a result of X-ray treatments to his face), he inevitably alienated himself with his sharp tongue and satiric wit from those who might be close to him.

WANDERING YEARS

Nonetheless Lewis was active during his years at Yale. He contributed freely to the *Courant* and the *Yale Literary Magazine* and enjoyed the respect of a few friends and professors. During the summers of 1904 and 1906, he visited England as a crewman aboard a cattleboat. At the close of his Junior year, dissatisfied with himself and with Yale, he left and spent a few months at Helicon Hall, Upton Sinclair's socialist colony in Englewood, New Jersey. He later attempted unsuccessfully to support himself as an editor and magazine writer. Finally in 1907, he returned to Yale and graduated in 1908.

EARLY WRITINGS

After graduation, still uncertain of what he wanted to do, Lewis wandered about the United States working at a variety of jobs. He worked for a time as a newspaper reporter and editor, and as an editor for various publishing houses, always continuously, but unsuccessfully writing short stories, poems and articles. By 1917, however, he had achieved some minor success. Always prolific, he had managed to sell some of his excess plot outlines to Jack London, and had numerous articles, poems, and short stories of his own published in numerous slick publications. And in addition to the *Hike and the Aeroplane* (1912), published under the pseudonym of Tom Graham, from 1914 to 1917, he published four novels: *Our Mr. Wren* (1914), *The Trail of the Hawk* (1915), *The Job*, and *The Innocents* (1917). Having thus achieved some small critical and financial success as a writer of potboiling romance, Lewis devoted his full time to his writing, and after another of this **genre**, *Free Air* (1919), he published the novel that was to make him famous, *Main Street* in 1920.

THE FABULOUS TWENTIES

Although Lewis' earlier novels had contained some of the seeds of his satiric genius, it was not until the publication of *Main Street* that he found his mark. Never before had an American author seriously questioned or challenged the failings of middle-class American life. The novel, first tentatively titled "The Village Voices" contained such a fiercely satiric attack upon the mediocrity of middle-class achievements and narrowness of middle-class beliefs that it provoked a storm of controversy unparalleled in twentieth-century American Literature. Nor did the controversy subside with the publication of *Babbitt* in 1922. For here again Lewis as a talented observer and recorder of American life had found his mark. Having first explored the dullness and drabness of small town life, Lewis now almost clinically recorded the life of the dull and bourgeois American businessman, George F. Babbitt, whose very name has become a synonym for all those who are limited, unimaginative, and functionless.

FAMOUS AT LAST

In 1925, now a successful and famous author, Lewis published *Arrowsmith* with the aid of researcher Paul de Kruif. Although Lewis intended the book to be idealistic and positive, in it he vented his ire upon the commercialism, quackery, pseudo-science, and glory hunting in medical education, medical practice, and medical research. Thus like its predecessors, *Arrowsmith* is both a **satire** and a social commentary on some essential aspect of American Life. Although *Arrowsmith* is regarded by many critics as Lewis' best book, Lewis refused the Pulitzer prize for it in 1926. Annoyed because *Main Street* and *Babbitt* had earlier been ignored, he denounced the prize, arguing that it was designed to make American writers "safe, polite, obedient, and sterile."

FAILURES OF THE TWENTIES

Although in the decade from 1920 to 1930 Lewis was to produce his best novels, it was not a decade without its failure. *Mantrap* (1926), a novel based on a vacation which Lewis had taken with his brother Claude, represented a return to this commercialism of his early novels. Slick, labored, and melodramatic, it was obviously a novel by which Lewis utilized his now considerable reputation to gather, as he put it, "some easy gravy." Lewis, however, quickly atoned for this retrogression with the publication of *Elmer Gantry* (1927), a violent study of religious fakery, and *Dodsworth* (1929), the sympathetic story of a man searching for fulfillment.

NOBEL PRIZE

In 1930, Sinclair Lewis was awarded the Nobel prize for literature. The first American ever to be so honored, he accepted the award proudly since the Nobel prize unlike the Pulitzer prize was not awarded for a single book, but for the entire body of his work. In his acceptance speech Lewis praised the work of fellow Americans, Theodore Dreiser, Thomas Wolfe, Thornton Wilder, John Dos Passos, Ernest Hemingway, and William Faulkner, and had prophetically named two future winners of the award, Faulkner and Hemingway.

THE DECLINE OF AN AUTHOR

With the decade from 1920 to 1930 over, Lewis, at the zenith of his career, was never again to produce work of the quality of *Main Street*, *Babbitt*, *Arrowsmith*, or *Dodsworth*. For the next twenty years, however, he was to continue writing novels, short stories, plays, and book reviews, and in addition, he was to be active as a teacher, lecturer, producer, and actor. Among the more notable of the novels of this period are *Ann Vickers* (1933), *It Can't Happen Here* (1935), *Cass Timberlane* (1945), and *Kingsblood Royal* (1947), all of which were either eventually produced on the State or made into movies.

PERSONAL LIFE

Although Lewis' professional life was a long and successful one, his personal life was not. Married during the early years of his struggle for recognition as a writer to Grace Hegger (1914), Lewis was for a time idyllically happy. However, in 1925, because of Lewis' growing irascibility, his addiction to alcohol, and the demands of his by now considerable fame as a writer, he and his wife separated and the marriage was terminated by divorce in 1928. Nor was his marriage to journalist Dorothy Thompson in 1928 to prove any more successful. From the beginning, Lewis' drinking and the clash of their careers made it impossible for the marriage to be successful. And again as he had in his first marriage, Lewis separated from his wife in 1937, and was divorced in 1942. Not even the fact that he had a son by each wife made marriage tenable for him. For like his relationship with his own father, Lewis was never able to successfully communicate with his own children. The first son, Wells, was killed in World War II and his second, Michael, incurred his father's displeasure by becoming an actor.

THE FINAL YEARS

During the last decade of his life, Lewis continued his tempestuous pace. Drinking heavily, and writing furiously, he formed a liaison with an actress considerably younger than himself, a relationship unfortunately no more satisfactory than his marriages had been. Finally in ill health and alone, he died in Rome on January 10, 1951, and his ashes were returned for burial to Sauk Centre where they were scattered over the fields of his birthplace. His last novel *World So Wide* was published posthumously later in that same year.

THE BACKGROUND OF BABBITT

Published in 1922, *Babbitt* was the first volume of what was later to be Sinclair Lewis' Zenith trilogy (the other two volumes are *Main Street* and *Arrowsmith*). Following the critical satiric method which had made him famous with the publication of *Main Street* in 1920, Sinclair Lewis now explored metropolitan America as he had small towns; he brought "Main Street" to the big city. In Zenith, an imaginary city in an imaginary state, located somewhere in America's Midwest, Lewis questioned through the medium of George F. Babbitt, a typical middle-class

American businessman, the attitudes, values, and beliefs long cherished by the American middle class.

By 1922, America, largely untouched by World War I, had just entered what was to be the "roaring twenties." It was the age of Warren G. Harding (1921–1923) and the return to "normalcy," an age of unparalleled prosperity for many, an age of optimism and boosterism, an age that was to end in the catastrophic depression of 1929.

It was also an age of revolt. Not only had many Americans traveled more widely as the result of the war and the automobile, but new scientific discoveries, an awakening of interest in and the extension of education for greater numbers of Americans, and the sharp probing and questioning of America's European expatriate writers had raised questions which were to challenge traditional American values. But here in Zenith, Lewis was to discover the last great bastion of conservative and traditional America still separated from the rest of the world geographically, morally, and intellectually; a stronghold of provincialism as yet safe from the rumblings of the flexible morality of the motor age, from the rootlessness of a mobile society, and as yet innocent of the complex nature of twentieth century existence.

As he had probed deeply small townism in *Main Street*, Lewis was to probe business ethics in *Babbitt*. Here insulated from the world, George F. Babbitt, like the numberless Babbitts of America, led a comfortable and secure existence, accepting almost without question, complacently, the vapid existence of the athletic club, the booster club, the lodge, the church social, and local culture society; and he remained only dimly aware of either the failure of the social order to provide adequately for all its citizens, or of the hypocrisy which was the essential characteristic of that order. Here the Babbitts of America lived blissfully unaware of the rise of Russian Communism, of Mussolini's dictatorship in Italy, or of the radical rumblings in America.

Here in Zenith a society yet existed which could complacently measure progress in purely material terms. Not only were the public buildings larger, but inexpensive, if shoddy; housing developments were springing up in all quarters. The range of interest of the Babbitts of America was here restricted to the arguments concerning the relative merits of septic tanks and sewers; to automobiles, houses, garages, as the status symbols of the successful. Here in Zenith was a society adrift, a society which measured progress by personal gain, judged the value of religious institutions by the size of their Sunday schools, evaluated its educational institutions by the size and equipment of their buildings; and finally, whose cultural societies could be measured by the incoherence of their leaders.

What then Lewis laid bare in *Babbitt* was not so much a man as an age. Nor did he perform that dissection with violence, but with love. For though Lewis satirized, chided, and exposed, he retained a fondness for George F. Babbitt because Lewis like most Americans realized there is a little Babbitt in all Americans. Nor has the age of Babbittry entirely passed, for greed, stupidity, and the desire for status are characteristics not only of Americans of the nineteen twenties, but of mankind.

Although much of Lewis' writing appears dated today because it appears to deal with a social order innocently remote from our own more sophisticated age, what Lewis contributed to American fiction with the writing of *Main Street* and *Babbitt* was a whole new subject matter for the novel. Although it is true that earlier novelists like Booth Tarkington, Frank Norris, and Jack London had explored economic America, none had explored it in such an individual, such a personal way. George F. Babbitt was not a special case, he was not an intelligent or sensitive man, alienated from his society, who regarded it from the heights and recorded its follies. George F. Babbitt was the common man, a participant in those follies and only dimly aware of the larger issues of the age. Nor did Sinclair Lewis propose any solutions to the follies which he recorded. It was enough to record them. For the satirist who is also a realist, the greater part of the solving of a problem is an awareness of its existence. What then *Babbitt* is, is a novel not intended to promote any political or social creed, nor to inspire some violent movement for reform, but a novel of awareness, a novel whose function in recording the sights and sounds of insular and provincial America was a prelude to change.

In *Babbitt* not only does the reader know what George F. Babbitt wears and does, but what he thinks, and, more importantly, what he doesn't think. The reader is a privileged witness to Babbitt's daily ablutions, petty jealousies, passionate longings, and vague unnameable fears, and through the medium of George F. Babbitt, the reader's own conscience is jogged, his own loyalties and biases questioned, and his own uncertainties voiced. Thus, although *Babbitt* at first seems a novel concerned with the mores of a particular time and place, it is in reality a novel whose concern is not only with business ethics and personal morality, but with the proper end of man.

A NOTE ON THE STYLE OF BABBITT

Babbitt is a typical modern novel in several respects, the most important of which is that it is virtually plotless. Although it is true that the novel contains elements of conflict and change, neither is of the variety to which the reader of earlier fiction was accustomed. First, the conflicts in which George F. Babbitt is

BRIGHT NOTES STUDY GUIDE

involved are only dimly perceived by him and are never resolved, although it is true that for a short time he reacts as a timid and uncertain rebel. Second, the plot of *Babbitt* does not contain the record of any particular or significant passage of time in the life of George F. Babbitt. The reader rather has the impression that the period covered by the novel might have been nearly duplicated by the recording of innumerable equivalent periods in Babbitt's adult life.

Thus, rather than a well-ordered plot which inexorably proceeds from incident to incident in strictly chronological order, *Babbitt* proceeds by a series of interludes of varying lengths and by means of which various aspects of George F. Babbitt and Zenith society are revealed. Indeed, perhaps the best way in which to fully illustrate the fragmentary approach to plot in *Babbitt* is revealed in the outline which follows.

Part I	A Typical Day In The Life Of George F. Babbitt	
	Chapter I	Morning
	Chapter II	Breakfast
	Chapter III	Babbitt drives to work
	Chapter IV	Morning at the office
	Chapter V	Lunch at the Athletic Club
	Chapter VI	Afternoon at the office
		Home for dinner
		Evening with Mrs. Babbitt and the children
	Chapter VII	Babbitt and Ted discuss education, success
		Evening at the Babbitts
		Evening in other parts of Zenith
Part II	The Babbitts Have Friends To Dinner	
	Chapter VIII	The guests

		The preparations
		The dinner and the after dinner diversions
	Chapter IX	Babbitt plays host
		The guests play games
		The guests depart

Part III   Babbitt And Paul Riesling

	Chapter X	The Babbitts visit the Rieslings
		Babbitt and Paul leave for Lake Sunasquam
	Chapter XI	Babbitt's and Paul's trip
		Their arrival and stay at Lake Sunasquam
		Their return to Zenith

Part IV   (An Interruption)

	Chapter XII	Some notes on Babbitt - the sportsman, the bridgeplayer, the conversationalist

Part V   Babbitt The Realtorltor, The Politician

	Chapter XIII	Babbitt at the State Realtors' Convention
	Chapter XIV	Babbitt's involvement in local politics

Part VI   The Dinner Parties

	Chapter XV	The college reunion
		The Babbitts invite the McKelveys to dinner
		The Overbrooks invite the Babbitts to dinner

Part VII   Babbitt The Churchman
             Chapter XVI   Babbitt and the Sunday School
                              Advisory Committee
             Chapter XVII   The committee plans its strategy

Part VIII   Babbitt, Verona, and Ted
             Chapter XIX   Ted and Eunice Littlefield Ted's
                              graduation party Mrs. Babbitt's
                              parents Babbitt's illness

Part IX   The Deal
             Chapter XIX   Babbitt and the tractor company
                              Babbitt and Ted, "The Babbitt Men"
                              Babbitt and Sir Gerald in Chicago
                              Babbitt's encounter with Paul

Part X   Babbitt And Paul
             Chapter XX   Babbitt, Paul and May Arnold in
                              Chicago Babbitt's attempt as
                              marriage counselor
             Chapter XXI   Babbitt and the Boosters
                              Paul shoots Zilla
             Chapter XXII   Paul's arrest, trial, and conviction

Part XI   Babbitt Alone - The Beginning Of Rebellion
             Chapter XXIII   Mrs. Babbitt leaves to visitrelatives
                              Babbitt seeks friends, diversions
             Chapter XXIV   Babbitt visits Paul at the penitentiary
                              Babbitt seeks feminine
                              companionship
                              The interlude with Ida
             Chapter XXV   Babbitt wonders
                              The vacation alone at Lake
                              Sunasquam

Chapter XXVI   The meeting with Seneca Doane
                The meeting with Zilla Riesling
                The argument at the Athletic Club
Chapter XXVII   The strike Babbitt becomes alienated
                    from his family and friends

Part X   Babbitt In Revolt
            Chapter XXVIII Babbitt meets Tanis Judique
            Chapter XXIX   Babbitt goes bohemian
                           The "Good Citizen's League" invites
                               Babbitt as a member
            Chapter XXX   Babbitt and Myra
            Chapter XXXI   Babbitt breaks with Tanis
            Chapter XXXII Babbitt rejects the "Good Citizen's
                               League"
            Chapter XXXIII Myra's Illness Babbitt returns to
                               the fold

Part XI   Conclusion
            Chapter XXXIV The "Good Citizen's League" spreads
                           Ted and Verona marry
                           Ted breaks the Babbitt mold

Thus *Babbitt* is a novel composed of a series of rather loosely organized scenes each of which provides a part of the total impression. If an organizing principle may be assumed to exist in *Babbitt* it is not based upon sequential narrative (though in general the scenes follow one another in a rough kind of chronological order), but upon the fact that George F. Babbitt is involved directly or indirectly in all of them. And although Lewis appears to tell all about George F. Babbitt during the course of the novel, actually he has carefully selected those activities and moments in Babbitt's life which reveal only those aspects of Babbitt's existence which Lewis wanted the reader to know. The result, of course, is that Babbitt emerges as a type more than an individual character, and an ideal embodiment of the social and economic order against which Lewis directs his satire.

Unfortunately the manner of Babbitt's characterization extends to other characters to which Lewis could not devote so much space. As a result such characters as Virgil Gunch, Orville Jones, William Eathorne, and Cecil Roundtree emerge only as lesser Babbitts. Indeed even those not immediately part of Babbitt's business world are embodiments of eternal Babbittry in their own spheres. Rev. John Jennison Drew is a religious Babbitt; Chum Frink a literary and intellectual Babbitt; Jake Offutt a political Babbitt; Joseph K. Pumphrey an educational Babbitt; Charles McKelvey a successful Babbitt; and Ed Overbrook a Babbitt who has failed.

Presented then in a welter of sharply realized detail *Babbitt* is a novel of **convention**, of social and intellectual sterility. It is at once a portrait and a criticism of a society whose values are a set of controlled and conditioned responses. Nowhere is there any meaningful activity, nowhere does any human communicate with another except through the medium of dehumanized **convention**. Babbitt does not advise Ted so that he may be happy, but so he may be successful. (The one jarring exception of course is at the novel's end.) The Boosters, The Good Citizen's League, the Church, and the Athletic Club are not institutions whose function is the betterment of mankind spiritually, ethically, or morally, but organizations whose functions are to produce conformity. Not even the so-called cultural organizations in *Babbitt* produce anything like communication, for their product is pseudo-intellectual fraud.

Of course Sinclair Lewis has, in a manner of speaking, stacked the cards against the forces of progress. For arrayed against the *Babbitt* legions are such ineffectuals as Seneca Doane, Paul Riesling, and Tanis Judique and her bohemian friends, with the result that Lewis somewhat characteristically overstates his case. However, it must be noted that *Babbitt* remains an exceptional artistic achievement. For not only does George F. Babbitt seem solidly real, but his very name remains as part of the American vocabulary.

Nor are overstatement and a tendency toward caricature Lewis' only faults in *Babbitt*. Its language and the speech of its characters are a true reflection of the uninspired and unimaginative middle-class Americans whom Lewis knew so well. Unfortunately with the passing of the era of which they were representative, so, too, have the colloquialisms and the **clichés** of their speech disappeared to be replaced by more modern equivalents - with the result that the book has a somewhat archaic flavor for the contemporary reader. Employing, often with great cleverness as well as veracity, **parody** and mimicry, Lewis recorded forever an age.

In addition to more or less direct commentary achieved through caricature and speech patterns, Lewis in *Babbitt* employed **irony** extensively. And although such **irony** is sometimes tedious as, for example, in the case of the contrasting dinners with the Overbrooks and the McKelveys, at other times it provides a brief and incisive commentary as, for example, when we are told that Babbitt was one of only nineteen speakers at Lucas Prout's victory dinner, or that the Reverend Drew's church was a true community center because it contained "everything but a bar."

No commentary on Lewis' style is complete unless it records the purpose of his writing. For although Lewis' style is flawed, no writer has more successfully recorded America and American attitudes. Recognizing early an America growing smug in her newly discovered strength as a result of World War I and unparalleled national prosperity, Lewis recorded that America's search for security and conformity. And through his often violent **satire** Lewis did much to bring about needed reforms. Indeed in some ways, then, Lewis as a recorder of his age might be compared to Dickens, for neither believed that change could be achieved through violent social upheaval but only through a change in the hearts and attitudes of individuals. And Lewis, writing in a prose style both journalistic and suited to the twentieth century, communicated to his reader an accurate and precise portrait of a civilization, a portrait which in many ways is still relevant. For although current status symbols may appear more sophisticated, and humans in general better educated than Babbitt, man's seeking after permanent and essential values remains a constant element of our social order.

And finally, if the measure of a writer may be determined by his influence and success, that is influence on other writers and success with a wide reading public, Lewis must be recorded as one of the pre-eminent American writers of the twentieth century.

BABBITT

CHAPTERS 1-6

....

| CHAPTER I

It is morning in Zenith, a city located somewhere in the great American Midwest, and George F. Babbitt awakens to the sounds of morning bustle in his home in the Floral Heights section of the city.

| Comment

The opening section of Chapter One is particularly prosaic. Filled with contrasts of beauty and ugliness, wealth and poverty, this section foreshadows the innumerable contrasts which are to follow. Zenith is a city "that seemed" made for laughter, and "it seemed" made for giants. As the reader soon discovers, Zenith like most things is not what it seems.

Arising fuzzily, Babbitt gazes out of his bedroom window at his corrugated iron garage. He then performs his customary morning ablutions in his porcelain and tile bathroom, and a short time later he engages in a protracted and oft repeated discussion with his now matronly wife, Myra, about wet bathroom towels and which suit he ought to wear.

Comment

The reader is immediately made aware that although *Babbitt* is a first person novel, dealing with subject matter largely hitherto untouched by the novelist, Lewis tells his story from the vantage point of the omniscient author. Not only is the reader told what Babbitt says and does, but what he thinks and feels. And further, like novelists of an earlier era, Lewis reserves the right to inject direct comment on the action, speech, or thought of his characters and thus direct the readers' attitudes.

In addition, an air of reality is created through the inclusion of innumerable details the accumulation of which provide an illusion of solidity, of actuality. It is through these details and Lewis' often ironic comments upon them that the novel achieves its satiric tone. For example, Babbitt's shoes are "standard," his spectacles of the "best glass," and the contents of his mind like his pockets are "ordinary." Thus an all pervading sense of the dullness of everyday Zenith existence is conveyed. Though the modern bathroom gleams, the razor is dull and the towels are wet. Though the breakfast is appetizing, Babbitt's digestion is impaired.

Finally, dressed in his grey suit with his Elk's tooth dangling from his watch chain and his pockets filled with the usual useless paraphernalia, Babbitt gazes out of his bedroom window at the gleaming towers of Zenith in the distance, his faith in the religion of business renewed. He then follows Myra down to breakfast.

Comment

The final section reveals Babbitt's all-pervading faith in an existence bounded completely by material objects. The shining modern bathroom and the gleaming Zenith towers are, of course, symbols of the sterile nature of that existence.

CHAPTER II

Babbitt's house and its furnishings are like Babbitt himself: glossy, comfortable, and moderately expensive. Its rooms were like the rooms of a good hotel: impersonal, standard. The only fault, Lewis reminds us, is that it is not a home.

Comment

Thus many of the attitudes of Chapter One are subtly reinforced. The house like the city of a false facade. Its furniture is very much like mahogany, its toilet articles made of almost silver; it is a modern house, a medium house, a standard house, an impersonal house, In all, it is a house which reflects the attitudes of its inhabitants who themselves have no artistic opinions and who are willing to accept in lieu the attitudes and values of decorators, builders, and maids.

At breakfast the family gathers. Verona, twenty-two, recently arrived from Bryn Mawr; Ted, seventeen, a high school student; and Tinka (Katherine), ten, the spoiled baby of the Babbitt family. As the family eats they discuss their various futures and argue over such mundane matters as the car, school, jobs, and what to wear. As usual, the earlier upset which Babbitt had experienced returns, and he turns for refuge to his morning paper, the

Advocate-Times, in which he searches in vain for solacing news or convenient attitudes which he may adopt as his own.

Comment

It is obvious that the Babbitt family, like the Babbitt home, is a model of standardization, a husband and wife, a boy and a girl. Nor are their minds any better furnished that their home. Their minds too are filled with standard notions and attitudes. Both Babbitt's and Ted's bad grammar are indications of the illiteracy which is possible even after years of formal education, and Verona's vague desire to do something worthwhile reveals her failure to have learned at college anything essential about the conditions of human existence.

The cursory and impersonal nature of the family conversation reveals a lack of the ability to communicate. Babbitt's concern with a vaguely defined socialism, Ted's concern with motor cars and movies, and Myra's concern with appearances reveal a shallow and somewhat selfish understanding of the purpose of existence. Neither Babbitt nor any member of his family has formulated a theory of living and neither, for that matter, had many of Lewis' readers.

Confused, tired, and angry, Babbitt nearly kisses Myra and leaves for the office, wondering vaguely whether his family and work are worth the effort they cost him.

Comment

The key to this chapter is, of course, not so much in the inconsistencies of Babbitt's attitudes and the rambling character of his thought, but in his lack of definitive conclusions. He has lately begun to wonder if the **conventions** which he has unquestionably accepted really matter.

CHAPTER III

On his way to work Babbitt greets a neighbor, Sam Doppelbrau, whom he regards as bohemian and a few moments later stops to talk to Howard Littlefield, PhD., publicity counsel for the Zenith Tractor Company. After an exchange of the usual **clichés** in which each confirms the other in the conventional opinions they share, Babbitt continues his drive to work filled with a sense of power and strength derived from his machine. After a satisfactory stop at his service station, Babbitt grandiloquently offers a lift to another businessman and finally he arrives at his office in the Reeves Building, a modern, efficient, and unornamented skyscraper in downtown Zenith.

Comment

As the name Babbitt is intended as a homonym for rabbit, a shy and unsure creature, so are the names of most of the novel's characters intended to reveal something about their characters. Sam Doppelbrau is of course a drinker. Howard Littlefield is a man who specializes in a narrow field but who pretends a wide knowledge of others, and Matt Penniman is a collector of small accounts.

As the members of the Babbitt household had largely failed to adequately communicate, so, too, do their immediate circle of friends and neighbors. They talk of the weather or exchange identical opinions on politics, business, and world affairs. Each is interested more in seeking the approval of his associates, inferior or superior, than he is in the search for the truth. Each is a citizen whose reputation is measured directly by his affluence. Each sees the universe as revolving about himself and his own small sphere of influence. And further, each takes satisfaction in the symbols of membership which are common to the group, the automobile one drives, the barbershop one frequents, the building in which one has his office, or the neighborhood in which one lives.

Babbitt, a partner in the Babbitt-Thompson (his father-in-law) Realty, is restless this morning and does not derive his customary satisfaction from his work. Attending to some details of his business distractedly, he lapses into daydreams about the fairy girl.

Comment

A new note has crept into Babbitt's life. Having reached a dangerous age, he begins to regret having spent so virtuous a life. With the coming of spring Babbitt again feels the awakening of his old romantic impulses.

CHAPTER IV

The morning progresses with the writing of bad advertisements for Glen Oriole and Linden Lane, a housing development and cemetery for which Babbitt and Thompson are agents.

Lewis here extends the scope of his **satire** with the inclusion of advertising. Though most of it is done in reality by the agents themselves, it is a model of the kind of misleading and deceptive advertising that is so common even now.

Having disposed of innumerable dull details of the morning's work, Babbitt again resolves to stop smoking and resorts again to one of the many schemes by which he hopes to stop. But, of course, he keeps right on smoking. Finally he calls Paul Riesling, who had been his roommate at college, and makes a luncheon date.

Comment

Babbitt's attempts to stop smoking represent one of Sinclair Lewis' defter and more realistic touches. Not only are the descriptions of Babbitt's many ridiculous schemes to stop smoking humorous, but they are common.

In many ways Babbitt was an ideal real estate man. He was as honest as was necessary, as virtuous as the necessities of respectability required, and as informed as his business required. He was hearty, bluff, confident, opinionated and, in general, ignorant. Yet Babbitt regarded himself as a good man because he contributed regularly to church and charity and because he lent his "vision" to the community's development as an ethical businessman.

Comment

Some of Lewis' most violent **satire** is contained in this chapter. For example, although Babbitt is against unions, he is not against unions for businessmen. Although he knows how much the local schools are worth, he does not know what goes on in them. And, although he believes himself honest, he condones vice and corruption as long as they don't affect him.

Babbitt closes the morning with a shrewd deal in which he and Conrad Lyte, a real estate speculator, force Archibald Purdy, a local butcher, to pay an exorbitant price for a lot next to his grocery.

Comment

Having first rather indirectly discussed Babbitt's business morality, Lewis provides in the last part of this chapter a concrete example in Babbitt's deal with Conrad Lyte.

CHAPTER V

After again breaking his resolution not to smoke, Babbitt leaves for the Zenith Athletic Club for lunch. As he drives there he contemplates the morning's profit and contentedly surveys with satisfaction the city of Zenith, carefully ignoring the slum areas.

Comment

Although Babbitt considers himself one of the builders of Zenith, one of the men of vision, the club to which he belongs is not very exclusive. We are told that it has three thousand members. The bad design of the club is of course matched only by the bad manners of many of its members.

At the club Babbitt is greeted by his friends, Vergil Gunch, Sidney Finkelstein, Joseph Pumphrey, all Boosters, or Elks, or both. Because Paul has not yet arrived, Babbitt spends a few minutes in conversation on a variety of topics which reveal both the ignorance and a general illiteracy of the participants. A short time later Paul arrives and he and Babbitt sit alone while Paul confesses his difficulties with his wife, Zilla. Finally, Babbitt and Paul devise a plan whereby they may escape the tedium of their wives for a few days' fishing in Maine.

Comment

The club, like so many aspects of Zenith life, is simply another status symbol. Here each member may for a time escape the realities of his existence, swap lies, and pretend he is something he is not. There are a number of clubs in Zenith all smaller and more exclusive than the Athletic Club.

Babbitt's friendship with Paul of course is real, and it is through the medium of this friendship that Lewis reveals the real human side of Babbitt so that the reader, like Lewis himself, never comes to hate or dislike Babbitt, but rather remains sympathetic toward him. The other members of Babbitt's business and social circle, excluding Paul, remain caricatures rather than fully drawn figures. Their conversation like much of the conversation between Babbitt and Paul is filled with clichés, localisms, and slang, much of which is now out-of-date.

CHAPTER VI

Returning to work, Babbitt visits a customer and later helps his father-in-law and partner Henry T. Thompson to buy a new car from Noel Ryland, a fellow Booster and sales manager for Zeeco cars.

Comment

Noel Ryland and Henry Thompson represent what Babbitt believes are the extremes of the business community, which has himself as the solid and common-sense center. In Babbitt's opinion, Thompson is crude and old fashioned while Ryland is artistic, too aesthetic. Each is actually a Babbitt of another generation, Thompson the Babbitt of the past, and Ryland the Babbitt of the future.

Later back at the office Babbitt finds it necessary to demonstrate with Stanley Graff, his outside salesman, for what Babbitt regard as a breach of business ethics. Graff asked for a raise.

Comment

Again Lewis uses a concrete example to demonstrate an argument which he has previously presented in more general terms. The actual nature of Babbitt's business ethics is not measured by morality, but by money. In some respects this scene is a bit heavy handed, yet the **irony** of Babbitt's remarks regarding love and marriage is effective.

After work Babbitt returns home, again greets Howard Littlefield and again engages with the family in the customary argument as to the relative merits of open or closed cars as status symbols. After dinner each resumes his customary evening activity, Ted his homework, Verona her social life, Myra her sewing, and Babbitt the comics.

Comment

Another aspect of Babbitt's life serves to reinforce the reader's awareness of its dullness.

There later ensues an involved discussion between Babbitt and Ted concerning the value of education. After a discussion of a variety of correspondence courses which Babbitt, like Ted, sees as practical, Ted finally agrees with his father that education could be improved if only educators would adopt the principles of efficient business management. Then Ted finally leaves to meet some friends without having finished his homework.

After Ted leaves, Babbitt and Myra discuss the children and reminisce about their own past. As they talk, Babbitt remembers that he had given up his dream of becoming a lawyer to marry Myra, and he becomes aware that their life together has been rather dull and routine. Even more surprising, he realizes that it has probably been that way for Myra, too.

Comment

Ted has unconsciously borrowed many of his father's attitudes even though Babbitt himself may not be aware of exactly what those attitudes are. Here Lewis chides the great American tradition of anti-intellectualism, a tradition which sees the function of the school to produce doers and makers rather than thinkers and artists. Ironically, the patently fraudulent advertisements which so captivate Babbitt and Ted are not dissimilar from the advertisements which Babbitt himself writes for his real estate.

BABBITT

....

CHAPTER VII

Later Babbitt and Myra leave the leaving room, exactly like most living rooms in Floral Heights, and go to bed. As Babbitt sleeps the scene changes to various other parts of Zenith where a murder is being committed, an evangelist is ending a tent meeting, a crooked political deal is being plotted, and a strike is being planned. And through it all, Babbitt dreams of his fairy girl.

Comment

Chapter Seven ends the first section of the novel, which presents a complete day from waking to retiring in the life of George F. Babbitt. It also serves as a transition for the section which is to follow, since many of the matters revealed at the chapter's close play an important part later in the novel.

The section of this chapter in which Seneca Doane and Dr. Yavitch discuss standardization contains the essence of Lewis' criticism of America. For like Doane, Lewis admires many of the very things which he opposes. Although he is aware of the sterility and dullness of standardization, he is not unaware of its benefits. And more, Lewis, like Doane, knew more about what he didn't want than what he wanted.

CHAPTER VIII

Having successfully bought in secret, some real estate options along a projected streetcar line before public announcement of its route, Babbitt decides to hold a dinner in celebration for some friends. After several weeks planning and debate, the guest list finally was complete and the dinner held. Among the more interesting preparations is Babbitt's securing the liquor from the local bootlegger who cheats him.

Comment

Again Lewis infuses some effective **irony**. After the care with which the guest list has been prepared, the selection of the most prosperous and respectable of Babbitt's friends, Babbitt goes to a bootlegger for the liquor they will all expect.

At the dinner the men joke manfully, drink their liquor, and approve prohibition because it keeps drink out of the hands of the lower classes. The meal, like the conversation, in uninspired. Chum Frink reads some of his latest poetry which the guests in their ignorant innocence admire, and with him they condemn all art which is not functional.

Comment

Again Lewis excoriates American anti-intellectualism. Bounded by the limits of his experience and intellect, the middle-class American has been taught to reject immediately anything which he cannot grasp. Chum Frink is, of course, a composite caricature of a number of popular newspaper poets of the 1920s, insipid, tasteless, unoriginal, but widely read and admired by an inadequately educated audience.

CHAPTER IX

What do we learn in the dinner party scenes

As the dinner progresses Babbitt enjoys playing host. However, uncomfortable because he has eaten too much, Babbitt is annoyed by Louetta Swanson's nagging of her husband, Eddie, and by his complaining. Later after a game of bridge, the guests engage in some spiritualist experiments which succeed in producing much crude humor among the men. Finally, after the usual discussions of the relative merits of automobiles, the guests depart.

Comment

The dinner, in spite of the elaborate preparations for it, is of course like so many of the Babbitt dinners in the past. The food, the guests, the games, and the conversations are almost identical.

After the guests have departed, Babbitt secures Myra's promise to help him convince Zilla to allow Paul to accompany him on the vacation to Maine. He then goes to bed, vaguely uncomfortable about his own impending freedom.

Comment

Babbitt is again true to type. Although he finds the routine of his life dull, the sudden prospect of freedom frightens him.

CHAPTER X

The Babbitts visit the Rieslings in their ultra-modern apartment in the Revelstoke Arms. Although the visit is for a while pleasant, Zilla reverts to her old habit of nagging Paul and they argue. Babbitt, angry, comes to Paul's rescue and demands that Zilla allow him to go to Maine. Zilla, cowed and contrite, finally agrees.

Comment

why Zilla such a negative character

Lewis' description of Zilla is both masterful and etched in acid. Zilla, like many middle-class housewives, has little to do, especially since she and Paul have no children - with the result that she takes out her frustrations on him. The argument in which they engage is an excellent example of Lewis' skill in writing realistic and effective dialogue.

After buying the necessary equipment, Babbitt and Paul leave by train. Filled with boyish enthusiasm, they join a group of businessmen in the smoking car, and while Paul reads, Babbitt joins in the customary discussions of such gatherings.

Comment

Here Lewis uses the smoking car as a kind of microcosm, or little world, which accurately reflects the larger world which

Smoking Car

he satirizes. The discussion of politics, business conditions, hotels, race, and national origin reveals compactly many of the targets which Lewis was to select for his **satire** in later novels. In general, the men in the smoking car are decent and hard working, but the opinions which they share are convenient, packaged, and conventional. They are opinions which they have never questioned, because they are the opinions of the age: opinions, born, bred, and nourished in a breezy and confident ignorance.

The final lapse of the conversation into off-color jokes is another realistic touch, and represents the desire of the group, since more conventional conversation has been exhausted, for a safe topic.

CHAPTER XI

Having twenty-four hours to wait in New York before their train leaves for Maine, Babbitt and Paul visit the Pennsylvania Hotel and the city docks where Paul momentarily contemplates leaving his unhappy life behind.

Comment

Lewis himself had often escaped the unhappiness of his life in travel. The **episode** at Lake Sunasquam is of course a middle-class idyll, the dream of escape, however temporary, from the tensions of everyday existence. The scene is reminiscent of many in Lewis' early adventure novels.

At the lake Babbitt and Paul luxuriate in an unfettered existence. The boat, fish, wander, and play poker with the guides.

But at the end of the first week their wives arrive, and the routines of marriage are soon re-established. When they return to Zenith, Babbitt is refreshed and confident about the future.

Comment

As the renewed Babbitt returns home, the reader is aware that his new resolve is no more durable than his resolve to stop smoking.

In this chapter, Lewis has humorously depicted the modern equivalent of the old romantic **cliché** of the restorative powers of nature. Babbitt, like so many Americans brought up on romantic poetry and adventure novels, believed implicitly in the therapeutic values of nature. Later in the novel, Babbitt will unsuccessfully attempt to find refreshment and renewed confidence as a result of a trip to the lake.

CHAPTER XII

Although he is filled with renewed faith in his capabilities, Babbitt soon returns to his former habits following his return to Zenith. Nor do his attempts to find solace in his usual recreations, bridge, baseball, movies, or conversation, do much to revive his waning spirits. He is somehow vaguely aware that this will prove to be a crucial year in his life.

Comment

Chapter Twelve is in the nature of an interruption of Babbitt's narrative, yet it provides a bridge for the material which is to follow. First, it enables the reader to see Babbitt in new perspective, in activities more remote from his business. And second, it increases our awareness of his new restlessness.

Lewis' depiction of Babbitt's fondness for baseball and movies, especially of bathing beauties, cowboys, and detectives, is, of course, another satiric comment on the intellectual and cultural nature of middle-class America's recreational preferences.

BABBITT

. . . .

CHAPTER XIII

Babbitt is invited to speak before the State Association of Real Estate Boards at their annual **convention** in Monarch because he has inadvertently impressed Cecil Roundtree, the delegation chairman, with his views on the dignity and value of the profession. His address is unexpectedly well received and he is appointed to a number of important committees. Happy over his success, Babbitt and some friends hold a celebration which Babbitt regrets as long as the hangover he has the next morning.

Comment

What does Babbitt say in his speech that is so successful

In this chapter Lewis invades another of the sanctuaries of business Babbittry, the **convention.** Not only does he evoke numerous ironic contrasts between the carefree, boisterous conventioneers and the other travelers on the train, but his description of the **convention** proceedings and the social activities which predominate is a masterpiece of satiric description. Babbitt's speech, which is so well received, is of course nothing more than a mouthing of an incredible series of clichés, nonsense, and disorganized trivia. That it is so well received by his fellow conventioneers is a sign that the sentiments which it expresses are conventional and safe, and therefore acceptable.

CHAPTER XIV

During the autumn elections Babbitt, mainly on the strength of his newly discovered eminence as a speaker, volunteers his services in the campaign of Lucas Prout, local candidate for mayor. Supported by virtually every business institution as well as both major political parties, Prout easily defeats Seneca Doane, the local attorney who has run on a pro-labor platform. Babbitt is rewarded for his services by being allowed to speak at a victory banquet, and by advance information concerning some new highways to be constructed within the city.

Comment

Prout is Lewis' idea of a pre-eminently safe candidate. Reasonably rich, he will not steal too much. Strangely, though Prout is supported by the respectable members of the community, including George F. Babbitt, it is respectable who are not above profiting from political victory.

A close reading of this chapter, however, reveals Lewis' belief that change is in the air. Though Prout and those like him are supported by the older members of the laboring class, the younger members of that class are staunchly for Seneca Doane.

Babbitt's speech before the Chamber of Commerce dinner celebrating Prout's victory is probably the best passage in the entire novel. It has often been quoted or reprinted separately as the essence of Babbittry. Disorganized, rambling, and filled with clichés, it extols the virtues of middle-class morality, of the standardized man, and of the standardized existence. It measures all human progress in purely material terms.

Now locally famous, Babbitt is invited to speak before various local organizations and his speeches are reported in the local papers.

CHAPTER XV

Babbitt's climb to local prominence is not without difficulties. He attends a reunion of his university class (1896) at the exclusive Union Club. Here the successful may be easily distinguished from the unsuccessful by the dress clothes or business suits they wear. Babbitt, dressed in evening clothes, wanders, shaking hands back and forth between each group. He finally wangles a seat alongside Charles McKelvey, a millionaire contractor, at dinner.

Comment

Social climbing takes many forms. Babbitt is frankly seeking social and business advantage at the class reunion. Lewis successfully recreates the forced cheerfulness, the dutiful notice of the unsuccessful on the part of the successful, and the pathetic attempts to recapture the past, which are the essence of all reunions.

As a result of the intimacy and good fellowship achieved at the reunion, the Babbitts invite the McKelveys to dinner and they accept. After many delays, the McKelveys arrive late, and, obviously bored by the whole proceeding, leave early. Though the McKelveys hold many dinners in the next few weeks, the Babbitts are not on the guest list.

Comment

The McKelveys are obviously a superior form of Babbitt and the two classes have nothing in common. Each class moves in its own circle, separated forever by differing interests and incomes.

The Babbitts, invited to dinner by the Overbrooks (an unsuccessful classmate), arrive late and leave early. Somehow the Babbitts never manage to invite the Overbrooks to dinner at their home.

Comment

The contrasting dinners provide a sharply ironic comment on the social aspects of Babbittry, for the Babbitts never realize that they have acted exactly as the McKelveys. This too is a good comment on the nature of humanity in general. Human beings are always much more aware of stupidity, vanity, and bad manners in others than they are in themselves.

CHAPTER XVI

Disturbed by his rejection by the McKelveys, Babbitt grows continuously more irritable, taking satisfaction only in the innumerable organizations to which he as a prominent citizen belongs.

Comment

Even Babbitt's reasons for belonging to so many fraternal organizations are not untinged by commercialism. He belonged, as did most of the other members of these organizations, because it was good for business.

Lewis' general analysis of the reasons for membership in such organizations constitutes the most violent attack on lodges ever made. He argued that most joined: because it was good for business; because it gave Americans an opportunity to adopt high-sounding titles; because it gave most an excuse to get out of the house at regular intervals; or because the lodge was a place where men could pretend to be men. Although Babbitt's primary reason for belonging was business, the other reasons were not unimportant to him.

Although Babbitt has not thought much about religion, he considers himself a Presbyterian primarily because he is a member of the Chatham Road Presbyterian Church. In reality his reasons for church membership are not unlike his reasons for lodge membership. Impressed by Reverend Drew, Babbitt decides suddenly to take a greater interest in church affairs.

Why be part of a church Religious hypocrisy

Comment

This chapter and the one which follows contain Lewis' first extensive treatment of the subject of religious hypocrisy which later forms the theme of his novel *Elmer Gantry* (1927). The Reverend John Jennison Drew is of course not an Elmer Gantry, but merely a religious Babbitt. He actually believes in what he is doing.

The church, like the lodge, in Lewis' view, had become simply another social organization where nothing essential or unpleasant was ever discussed. The success or failure of a church could be measured by the size of its membership, and a churchgoer measured by the regularity of his attendance rather than by the sincerity of his belief. Nor was Babbitt too different from most churchgoers. His hazy belief in the respectability of religion, of the efficacy of the Golden Rule, and of the existence of heaven, even if he wasn't too sure about hell, conveys effectively Lewis' idea of the middle-class American concept of religion.

CHAPTER XVII

Babbitt, "Chum" Frink, and William Eathorne, president of the First National State Bank of Zenith, now members of a Sunday School Advisory Committee, plan a campaign to secure members for the Sunday School with the aid of Kenneth Escott, reporter for the *Advocate-Times*. Their program proves a great success. It is even more successful later, because Babbitt is able to borrow money from Eathorne for a shady deal, and because Escott marries Verona.

Comment

Not only does Lewis depict the church as vapid and superficial, but he believes that its pillars are often corrupt. Ironically, Babbitt and Eathorne, who proclaim the church as the refuge of the respectable, are not themselves above a shady deal. And further, Babbitt's plan, which so successfully enlarges the Sunday School through games and prizes, has effectively demonstrated that business and religion have a common ground, there is a profit to be made in each.

CHAPTER XVIII

Babbitt is an average father. Although he knows how much his children spend, he knows little else about them. Verona has lately become seriously involved with Kenneth Escott, and Ted, though a good athlete, is doing poorly in school. At a party for Ted and his classmates, Babbitt is shocked to discover that the young people drink and smoke.

Comment

Again Lewis illustrates the serious lack of communication which exists between one generation and another.

The evening a week Babbitt must spend with Myra's parents, the embarrassments of his mother's and his half-brother Martin's visits, all serve to increase Babbitt's irritability. Although Babbitt enjoys the attentions he receives because of an illness in February, his recovery revives his dissatisfaction with the routine of his life.

Comment

Again Lewis uses the device of parallel narrative to reinforce a point. As Ted and Verona resent Babbitt's and Myra's attempts to understand them, so, too, Babbitt and Myra resist such attentions on the part of their own parents.

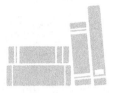

BABBITT

CHAPTER XIX

The Street Traction Company deal is finally closed, enabling Babbitt to realize a three-thousand-dollar profit. Babbitt's satisfaction is marred by the discovery that Stanley Graff, his outside salesman, is dishonest, so Babbitt fires him.

Comment

Actually Babbitt's objection to Graff's double dealing on the house leases provides Babbitt with an opportunity to re-establish some of the principles which he had compromised in the Traction deal. In addition, he objected to the fact that most of the profit from Graff's deal would have gone to Graff and not Babbitt and Thompson. If there was anything Babbitt could not stand, it was being cheated.

Babbitt takes Ted on a business trip to Chicago where they develop a closer relationship than they have ever shared before. After Ted leaves, a chance meeting with Sir Gerald Doak provides Babbitt with considerable satisfaction. Several evenings later, however, Babbitt is shocked to meet Paul Riesling in the company of May Arnold, an unattractive middle-aged woman.

Comment

Paul's story represents what is as near to a plot as the novel contains.

CHAPTER XX

Paul confides to Babbitt his intimacy with May Arnold. Although Babbitt is dismayed, he agrees to help Paul keep his secret. Later, back in Zenith, Babbitt visits Zilla and manages to secure from her a promise to be a better wife. Although relations between Paul and Zilla improve, Paul believes it is too late.

Comment

Babbitt's attempts as mediator, though sincere, are ineffectual. Unable to fully understand himself completely, he is baffled by Paul and Zilla.

In this chapter and the one which precedes, Lewis advanced his somewhat halting plot through the device of coincidence. It is, of course, highly unlikely that Babbitt would so conveniently meet Sir Gerald Doak and Paul Riesling in Chicago.

CHAPTER XXI

Shortly after Babbitt is elected vice president of the Zenith Boosters Club, he receives the news that Paul has shot Zilla.

Comment

Paul's shooting of Zilla is crucial in Babbitt's life, since Paul is in reality Babbitt's only friend. Babbitt cannot, and indeed has never, contemplated life without Paul, and the sudden prospect of the loss of Paul's friendship forces Babbitt to think seriously of what is important in his life.

CHAPTER XXII

Babbitt is allowed to visit Paul in jail through the influence of Mayor Lucas Prout, but he can do nothing. Although he fears Paul's action will disgrace him at the Athletic Club, the men there say nothing. Zilla recovers, but Paul is sentenced to three years in prison.

Comment

Babbitt's worst fears are now realized. He has lost Paul and is now adrift. Babbitt's willingness to perjure himself for Paul effectively demonstrates the depth of feeling of which he is on occasion capable and enables the reader to maintain a sympathetic attitude toward him, despite his often shallow and dishonest behavior.

CHAPTER XXIII

During the months which follow, Babbitt tries to lose himself in a variety of activities. He is especially lonely when Myra and Tinka leave to visit some relatives in the east. Nothing, however, seems effective. Finally, reviewing his life, he decides to become a rebel. He first asserts his new independence by leaving the office during working hours and in unsuccessful flirtations with Miss McGoun, his stenographer, and later with Louetta Swanson.

Comment

Confused and lonely, Babbitt finds little satisfaction in his usual activities. Unfortunately, his rebellion against the routine of his customary life is too late.

CHAPTER XXIV

Saddened and lonely after a visit to Paul at the penitentiary, Babbitt is revived by a mild flirtation with Tanis Judique, a woman who rents an apartment from him. Emboldened by the success of his flirtation with Tanis, he makes a date with Ida Putiak, a manicurist in his barbershop. Unfortunately, he is too old and she is too disinterested.

Comment

Babbitt's first real foray into rebellion is an unqualified failure.

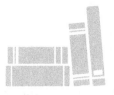

BABBITT

CHAPTER XXV

Although the next morning Babbitt awakens doubtful of his rebellion, he feels certain that somewhere there exists a woman who will understand and love him. When Myra returns in August, he is uncomfortably aware that he has not missed her.

Hoping that a vacation in Maine alone will restore his flagging spirits, Babbitt departs for Lake Sunasquam. Unfortunately he cannot recapture the happiness he had experienced here on his last trip with Paul, and so he leaves for Zenith.

Comment

Babbitt discovers that he cannot find happiness in his attempts to relive the past. This chapter contrasts sharply with Chapter Eleven in which Babbitt was rejuvenated by a trip to the lake.

CHAPTER XXVI

On the train home Babbitt meets Seneca Doane, who like Paul had been a college classmate, and discovers that they have much in common.

Comment

Babbitt, of course, had avoided Seneca Doane for years because Doane had a reputation as a radical. And though Babbitt, like many members of his class, has long regarded Doane as some sort of monster, he is somewhat surprised to discover that Doane is quite human.

Babbitt calls on Zilla but fails to produce any change in her by now hardened attitude toward Paul. In addition, she has become a religious fanatic. Later Babbitt, still unsettled, startles his friends at the Athletic Club by his defense of Seneca Doane. Meanwhile, Ted, now at the State University, seeks Babbitt's permission to change to the school of engineering, but Babbitt refuses.

Comment

In this chapter Lewis provides information which foreshadows not only the extent and nature of Babbitt's rebellion in the future, but Ted's as well.

CHAPTER XXVII

In September a series of strikes breaks out in Zenith which engender much hard feeling. Babbitt, to the surprise of his friends, defends both Seneca Doane and the strikers. He even challenges the view of Reverend Drew who has delivered a sermon against the strike.

Comment

Because most of the members of the Chatham Presbyterian Road Church are members of the business community, Reverend Drew's defense of their position is not surprising.

When the strikers are finally dispersed by the National Guard, Babbitt's defense of the strikers alarms his friends, who fear his is becoming a radical. Nor is his family sympathetic to his new views which they cannot share nor understand.

Comment

Rarely in times of crisis is it possible for men to achieve the objectivity for which Babbitt so strenuously argued. The scenes of the Zenith strike and of the National Guard's intervention represent Lewis' satiric commentary on yet another aspect of the American scene during the nineteen twenties.

CHAPTER XXVIII

Tanis Judique calls on Babbitt at his office and the two soon become fast friends. Because she is understanding, Babbitt agrees to have dinner at her apartment.

Comment

Tanis now provides the sympathetic understanding for which Babbitt has yearned since Paul was imprisoned. More importantly, she restores some of the confidence which he has lost because of the conflicts with his friends and family.

CHAPTER XXIX

Alienated from his acquaintances at the Athletic Club because of his radical opinions, Babbitt spends more and more time with Tanis and her bohemian friends.

Comment

Having lost the approval of his former friends, Babbitt finds it necessary to seek approval by Tanis and her friends.

When Myra leaves town again to care for her sick sister, Babbitt's involvement becomes more complete. Drinking heavily, Babbitt spends almost every evening with Tanis and her friends. And although he now finds his former friends uninteresting, he discovers a new friend in Sam Doppelbrau, his bohemian neighbor.

Comment

As Zilla had been converted wholeheartedly to "religion," so, too, Babbitt has become a convert to his new way of life.

One day Vergil Gunch invites Babbitt to join a newly formed chapter of the Good Citizen's League. Though confused and worried by Gunch's threats of what will happen to those who don't join, Babbitt remains noncommittal.

Comment

The Good Citizen's League is actually a pressure group whose primary purpose is to enforce conformity to their views. The 1920s abounded in such groups which often claimed large memberships. Probably the most infamous and least subtle of such groups was the Ku Klux Klan.

CHAPTER XXX

After Myra's return, Babbitt, feeling guilty, tries to treat her more considerately. However, since he is unwilling to break with Tanis, his attempts are unsuccessful. Finally, after a violent argument, Babbitt fearfully begins to reconsider his new way of life.

Comment

The New Thought League whose lectures Myra and Babbitt attend represents Lewis' satiric view of the many local cultural societies which were popular in America. Actually in this instance the league is a new form of fraud which makes it money from ignorant and unsophisticated middle-class Americans who have been led to believe that the league can help them to find happiness. Borrowing freely from various religions, and philosophic systems, the league's teachings are a hodgepodge of nonsense.

CHAPTER XXXI

Shocked at his own treatment of Myra, Babbitt discovers that upon reflection she is a far superior person to Tanis or any of her friends. As a result, he finally breaks with Tanis, though not without one more visit during which he is surprised to find that he actually preferred Myra to Tanis.

Comment

At least one aspect of Babbitt's rebellion has ended.

CHAPTER XXXII

Babbitt tells Myra of his involvement with Tanis and manages to make her feel that it has been all her fault.

Later that week Babbitt challenges the opinions of a guest speaker at the Boosters Club luncheon, and a short while after refuses to join the Good Citizen's League in spite of threats from Charles McKelvey, Dr. Dilling, and Colonel Snow, owner of the *Advocate-Times*. Soon he finds that his friends are avoiding him and that his business is losing customers. Frightened, he wishes for another opportunity to join the league.

Comment

Babbitt's rebellion is nearing an end. Pressured now on all sides and alone, he finds himself on unfamiliar ground.

CHAPTER XXXIII

Babbitt, fearful and frightened, wonders how he can end his rebellion and still maintain his dignity. Suddenly one night Myra is taken ill and must be removed to a hospital. Following a serious operation which is successful, Babbitt pleads for her forgiveness.

As a result of Myra's illness old friends suddenly begin to call again and Babbitt is again given an opportunity to join the league, which he does eagerly.

Comment

Fate has provided Babbitt with a dignified means of returning to the fold of the conventional.

CHAPTER XXXIV

The Good Citizen's League spreads; Babbitt returns to the church, the Boosters, the Elks, and the Athletic Club. Verona marries Kenneth Escott; Ted marries Eunice Littlefield and leaves college; and Babbitt, back in the good graces of the city administration, is invited to another deal with the Traction Company.

Comment

Although *Babbitt* does not contain a plot in the conventional fashion, Babbitt as **protagonist** has come full circle. He began as a conventional, standardized man, ventured into discontent and rebellion, and has now returned to the fold. However, Babbitt's advice to Ted to do what he thinks best with his life is a sign that he has grown. Although he will, in general, live in accordance with the **conventions** of the middle-class world, he will not do so without question.

BABBITT

CHARACTER ANALYSES

58 Characters

....

Because *Babbitt* is a novel which records an age as well as a few months in the life of George F. Babbitt, it is a novel which contains a great number of characters. Although admittedly a large number of these characters are introduced only briefly, and an almost equally large number are very sketchily drawn, all are important to the development of the novel as a realistic re-creation of that age.

Even George F. Babbitt is not fully realized, despite the fact that the reader is presented with an awesome quantity of information about him. For although Sinclair Lewis in creating Babbitt seems to tell us all, he actually carefully selects those details and moments in Babbitt's life which reveal only those aspects of Babbitt's character which are useful in the development of the novel. In any case, Babbitt does emerge as a recognizable type with whom the reader is able to sympathize.

Thus, *Babbitt* is a novel filled with a variety of characters: doctors, lawyers, ministers, realtors, bootleggers, hunting guides, salesmen, politicians, newspapermen, and college professors, and many made more immediately recognizable because Lewis attempted to find names which revealed some significant aspect of each character. For example, Howard Littlefield, Ph.D. is a man who has mastered a narrow field though he has pretensions to wider knowledge. Matt Penniman is a collector of small accounts, and ironically, Barnabas Joy is a Zenith undertaker.

MAY ARNOLD

An unattractive middle-aged woman with whom Paul Riesling has an affair in Chicago.

GEORGE F. BABBITT

A typical middle-aged American businessman. At forty-six he is a partner in the reasonably successful realty firm of Babbitt and Thompson. Vaguely dissatisfied, he has lately begun to question the conventions, the values, and the mores of his ordered existence, and of those of the society of which he is a part. Although often sketchily drawn, he emerges as a sympathetic, if confused, human being. Though for a time he revolts against **convention**, the revolt is doomed to failure because he is inadequately prepared to be anything but what he now is. In addition, though Lewis often violently condemns most of the attitudes, institutions, and **conventions** for which Babbitt stands, he never loses his sympathy for Babbitt the man.

MYRA BABBITT

Babbitt's drab and middle-aged wife who accepts unquestioningly the **conventions** of her standardized existence. With even less imagination than Babbitt, she cannot understand his disquieting attempts to escape, nor is she competent to guide and counsel the children.

THEODORE (TED) ROOSEVELT BABBITT

Babbitt's son. He is in many ways a typical teenager. Although he appears to be in revolt, he is actually conforming to the **conventions** of his generation as Babbitt did to his. A poor student, he is more interested in mechanics and his social life than he is in school. He later quits college to work as a mechanic and elopes with Eunice Littlefield.

KATHERINE (TINKA) BABBITT

At ten, the spoiled baby of the Babbitt family.

VERONA BABBITT

Babbitt's eldest daughter. Having recently graduated from Bryn Mawr, she is employed as a file clerk at the Gruenberg Leather Company, a job eminently suited to her meager talents. Still largely uneducated in spite of her college degree, she yearns to do something worthwhile with her life though she hasn't the slightest idea what. She later marries her male counterpart, Kenneth Escott, reporter for the *Advocate-Times*.

MISS WILBERTA BANNIGAN

File clerk and accountant for Babbitt-Thompson Realty.

MISS ELNORA PEARL BATES

Society editor for the *Advocate-Times.*

FULTON BEMIS

A member of Tanis Judique's "bunch" and a railway clerk who is temporarily Babbitt's "rival" for Tanis.

THOMAS BYWATERS

Babbitt's part-time salesman who is a full-time streetcar conductor.

DR. A. I. DILLING

A local surgeon, an important member of the Boosters Club and a leader in the Good Citizen's League.

SIR GERALD DOAK

British industrialist for a time a guest of the McKelveys. Babbitt's chance meeting with him in Chicago reveals another side of his character.

SENECA DOANE

Former college classmate of Babbitt who has become a lawyer associated with radical and humanitarian causes.

REVEREND JOHN JENNISON DREW

Pastor of the Chatham Road Presbyterian Church. His businesslike approach to religion appeals to Babbitt.

CLARENCE DRUM

Local shoe merchant who acts as a captain in the local unit of the National Guard during the general strike.

WILLIAM E. EATHORNE

President of the First National Bank of Zenith and an influential man who is impressed by Babbitt's work on the Sunday School Committee.

KENNETH ESCOTT

Reporter for the *Advocate-Times*. After he helps Babbitt with the publicity for the Sunday School Committee, he becomes engaged to Verona and they later marry. Like her, though college educated, he is superficial and a shallow thinker.

SIDNEY FINKELSTEIN

A friend of Babbitt and a fellow Booster and Athletic Club member, and a buyer for Parcher & Stein's Department Store.

T. CHOLMONDELEY FRINK (CHUM)

A friend and neighbor of Babbitt. Advertising copywriter and syndicated poet. He represents Lewis' satiric jab at a number of nationally prominent newspaper poets.

STANLEY GRAFF

Babbitt's outside salesman. He often clashes with Babbitt and is finally fired for "unethical" business practices.

VERGIL GUNCH

A friend of Babbitt, he is a local coal dealer, president of the Zenith Boosters, leader of the Zenith Elks, and one of the leaders of the Good Citizen's League. He is a kind of super-Babbitt.

WILLIS IJAMS

President of the Zenith Boosters following the resignation of Vergil Gunch.

BEECHER INGRAM

Former minister of the Congregational Church now associated with Seneca Doane and various humanitarian causes.

ORVILLE JONES

A friend of Babbitt and owner of the Lily White Laundry, largest in Zenith.

TANIS JUDIQUE

A middle-aged, but captivating widow with whom Babbitt for a time becomes involved. Although she is a member of a bohemian group, her way of life, like Babbitt's, is circumscribed by the **conventions** of the group.

CHESTER KIRBY LAYLOCK

Salesman for Babbitt-Thompson Realty stationed at the company's development, Glen Oriole.

EUNICE LITTLEFIELD

Daughter of Howard Littlefield. A young, gum-chewing, movie-going teenager. She and Ted Babbitt later marry.

HOWARD LITTLEFIELD

A friend and neighbor of Babbitt. Because he holds a Ph.D. in Economics, he is considered by his friends as an expert in all matters. He, of course, shares their opinion of his infallibility.

MARTIN LUMSON

Rival realtor and developer of Avonlea in competition with Babbitt's Glen Oriole.

CONRAD LYTE

Real estate speculator for whom Babbitt acts in the deal with Archibald Purdy, a local grocer.

P. J. MAXWELL

Defense attorney for Paul Riesling after he shoots Zilla.

THERESA MCGOUN

Babbitt's attractive stenographer.

CHARLES MCKELVEY

Former classmate of Babbitt and now a millionaire contractor. Babbitt's attempt to re-establish their college friendship is unsuccessful. He later becomes a leader in the Good Citizen's League.

LUCILLE MCKELVEY

Wife of Charles McKelvey, and a leader of Zenith's society.

MIKE MONDAY

An evangelist preacher. Although he never appears, he probably represents Lewis' caricature of the famous evangelist, Billy Sunday.

SYLVESTER MOON

Mechanic and gas-station attendant at the garage which Babbitt patronizes.

OPAL EMERSON MUDGE

Leader in the Zenith chapter of the New Thought League.

CALEB NIXON

Colonel of the Zenith National Guard and secretary of the Pullmore Tractor Company.

CARRIE NORK

A member of Tanis Judique's bohemian "bunch."

JAKE OFFUTT

Owner of a local car body works, and local political boss.

ED OVERBROOK

A former classmate of Babbitt at State University who has failed in business. The dinner to which he invites Babbitt is unsuccessful as the Babbitt's dinner for the McKelveys was unsuccessful.

JOE PARADISE

Babbitt's guide at Lake Sunasquam, who would rather play poker than guide.

LUCAS PROUT

A local manufacturer whom Babbitt helps in a successful mayoralty campaign against Seneca Doane.

PROFESSOR JOSEPH K. PUMPHREY

A friend and fellow Booster of Babbitt, owner of the Riteway Business College.

ARCHIBALD PURDY

A local grocer who is bested in a real estate deal by Babbitt and Conrad Lyte.

IDA PUTIAK

A young manicurist at the Pompian barbershop in the Hotel Thornleigh.

PAUL RIESLING

Babbitt's oldest and closest friend. A shy, sensitive man, he feels trapped by his work and by his marriage.

ZILLA RIESLING

Paul Riesling's shrewish wife. Childless and unhappy, she blames Paul for all the failures of their married life. Following her recovery after Paul shoots her, she turns to religious fanaticism.

CECIL ROUNDTREE

A competitor of Babbitt and leader of the Zenith Delegation to the S.A.R.E.B. **convention** in Monarch.

NOEL RYLAND

Sales manager for Zeeco Cars and fellow member of the local Boosters.

SHELDON SMEETH

Education Director of the Y.M.C.A. and choir director of the Chatham Road Presbyterian Church.

COLONEL RUTHERFORD SNOW

Owner of the *Advocate-Times*, Zenith's largest newspaper, and a leader of the Good Citizens League.

EDDIE SWANSON

A fellow-member of the Athletic Club, and neighbor and agent for Javelin Motor Cars.

LOUETTA SWANSON

Wife of Eddie Swanson. A bored, flighty woman who constantly nags her husband. Babbitt flirts with her once unsuccessfully, but is complimented on his improvement on a second occasion following his affair with Tanis.

HENRY T. THOMPSON

Babbitt's father-in-law and partner in the Babbitt-Thompson Realty Co.

HORACE UPDIKE

Zenith's professional bachelor and philanderer.

FRITZ WEILINGER

The salesman whom Babbitt hires to replace the fired Stanley Graff. As the name implies, he is more willing than Stanley.

DR. KURT YAVITCH

Radical scientist and friend of Seneca Doane.

BABBITT

Among the most successful and famous of Sinclair Lewis' novels, *Babbitt* is superior to most of Lewis' other novels in the creation of the character George F. Babbitt, realtor. Dealing in great detail with the surface of a large portion of American life, the novel explores a society devoted to boosterism, pep, gadgetry, and joinerism. And although the portrait of that society is satiric and often exaggerated, it is not inaccurate. Including a great number of characters, and ranging widely over an extensive canvas, the novel exposes the vulgarity, the foolishness, the stultification of the morality and the **conventions** of that society.

The novel's **protagonist**, George F. Babbitt, is an ordinary man, a standard man. He represents the average upper-middle-class American businessman whose ethics and thoughts are bounded by the limits of the society of which he is a typical representative. Engrossed by gadgets, he possesses the latest in alarm clocks, cigar cutters, and cigar lighters for his car. His home is filled with standardized and mass-produced bric-a-brac, and is adorned and decorated according to the latest decrees of those faceless and nameless persons whose function it is to decree and decorate the homes of those unwilling or unable to do so for themselves.

The novel opens in Floral Heights, an upper-middle-class housing development three miles from the center of Zenith, the state's second largest city. Here, George F. Babbitt lives with his wife, Myra, and his children, Verona, Ted, and Tinka. They, like Babbitt, exist as part of a society whose boundaries are defined by limits of the neighborhood and the city which they inhabit, and the traditions and **conventions** which they have inherited.

Babbitt and Myra, married during their years together at State College where Babbitt had once idealistically hoped to become a lawyer, have drifted aimlessly through some twenty-five years of married life. It is doubtful whether they have ever been able to communicate with one another because their marriage has been accepted by Babbitt with the same stoicism and lack of imagination which are the chief characteristics of his mental and emotional attitudes. Like his business, like his clubs, Myra is merely part of the machinery of his existence, a situation which she only dimly understands, but uncomplainingly accepts.

It is, however, Babbitt's business life which is the novel's chief concern. Long a partner with his father-in-law, Henry Thompson, in the firm of Babbitt and Thompson, Babbitt has been moderately successful. He has achieved a standard of living somewhat above the average by adopting, without question, as he adopts most of the **conventions** of existence, the dubious morality of the business world which he sees around him. Although he considers himself ethical and honest, he is not above making a profit from a shady deal because he believes that if he doesn't realize that profit, someone else will. Although often vaguely uncomfortable about the possible immorality of his dealings and vaguely uncomfortable about their legality, he justifies them with the argument that he has never done anything which wasn't necessary to the advancement of progress. Of course, like most men, he tends to measure the march of progress in terms of his own gain.

Babbitt also belongs to innumerable business and fraternal organizations, primarily because they are a means of furthering his business. He is a member of the Elks, the local chapter of the Boosters, the Athletic Club, the State Board of Realtors, and the Republican party. Not only does belonging to such organizations satisfy his gregarious nature, but it provides him with further proof of his prominence in the community and a sense of belonging. Unfortunately, Babbitt, like most other members of these organizations, is only dimly aware of the purposes of these organizations other than the belief that they exist to somehow further the ideals of America and of the business community, which is the heart of America. It does not strike Babbitt as strange that almost the same group of members appears to belong to each of the organizations to which he belongs. Nor does it appear to him unusual that the purpose of most of these organizations is identical: to line the pockets of, and to dictate and standardize the beliefs and ethics of all those who belong to them as well as of as many others whom they can influence or intimidate.

Not only is Babbitt a businessman, but he is an employer, and as a good employer he seeks to establish the patterns of ethical business practice and to secure the undying loyalty of all who work for him. Unfortunately he often succeeds all too well. Though most of his employees endure him, Stanley Graff, his outside salesman, subscribes wholly to Babbitt's creed. He adopts Babbitt's dubious ethics and pretends to believe in the religion of business because he has observed at first hand that this lights the road to success. Too late he discovers that the cardinal sin for those who engage in unethical practices is to be caught.

Although Babbitt is a church member (this, too, is good for business), he is doubtful about what he really believes. Only sure that there is a heaven, he entertains doubts about hell. He is, however, vaguely aware that the church's function is to provide guidance for children (through the Sunday school at least), and to act as a civilizing agency among those who without its stabilizing influence would be liable to err. Though he drinks, and he approves of drinking for his friends, he has adopted his church's stand for Prohibition on the grounds that since bootleg liquor is more expensive than legal liquor, Prohibition tends to keep it out of the hands of the lower classes. He, like the pastor and most of the other members of the church to which he belongs, believes that the effectiveness of a church can be measured by the number and influence of its parishioners.

Babbitt is a staunch supporter of education. Himself a graduate of the State University where he received his degree in Sociology, he has maintained untouched the natural ignorance preferred by the class to which he belongs. He has long, as a businessman, been aware of how much school buildings cost, how much they are insured for, but does not know how much teachers are paid, what their qualifications are, or exactly what goes on inside the school. Through Ted and Verona, Tinka and his own memories, he suspects that the schools spend too much time attempting to inculcate a respect for culture and an understanding of literature in the young, rather than spending more time teaching than some practical means of making a living.

Nearly every evening of his life Babbitt spends a portion of his time perusing the *Advocate-Times*. Here he finds both entertainment in the comic strips and edification in the editorials and news whose opinions he may conveniently adopt as his own. He reads the *Advocate-Times* almost exclusively because he can be reasonably certain that its opinions and concepts are almost certain to conform to his own long held and cherished prejudices. How extensive the practice of Babbittry is in Zenith may be gleaned from the information that the *Advocate-Times* was the city's largest and most influential newspaper.

It is true, however, that Babbitt's gregarious nature is not entirely satisfied by his membership in innumerable organizations. He is a friendly man, a good neighbor, and a good host. In fact, when he has an occasion to celebrate, he finds enormous satisfaction in inviting a group of his friends to dinner. Of course, it is very likely that the group which he assembles on these festive occasions, as for example following the securing of leases in the Traction Company deal, is likely to prove the same group of friends and business acquaintances whom he invites to most of his dinners. It is also likely that the menu, the conversations, the games, and the flirtations will strongly resemble most of the dinners which he gives or attends. The truth is that although Babbitt calls Vergil Gunch, Sidney Finkelstein, Howard Littlefield, Orville Jones, and Eddie Swanson friends, they are actually only business acquaintances or neighbors whom he invites because they belong to the same social strata as himself.

In spite of Babbitt's tendencies toward a social gregariousness strongly tinged by desire for social and financial gain, he is not incapable of real friendship. For many years he has maintained a real and steadfast friendship with Paul Riesling, a former college classmate who is now a Zenith roofing dealer. Attracted to each other in college because each was shy and idealistic, they have remained intimate even though Babbitt has changed to completely conform with the patterns required by **convention**, and has remained sensitive, idealistic, and unhappy because he cannot completely rebel against the constrictions of his business or his marriage. The friendship of Babbitt and Paul is in many ways a strange one, a friendship of opposites. Their friendship is reinforced by the sanction of long duration, with the result that Babbitt and Paul supplement each other; each supplies that portion of character which is missing in the other. It is not then surprising when Babbitt's vague feeling of dissatisfaction becomes open rebellion after Paul is imprisoned for shooting Zilla, because Babbitt lost not only Paul's companionship, but an essential part of himself.

Babbitt is also a lover of the great outdoors. Periodically in need of refreshment, he looks forward to his vacation in the wilds of Maine at Lake Sunasquam where he may hunt, fish, and loaf, and more importantly, lie, swear, and play poker with the guides. This is the escape which he has long been taught is both the necessity and the prerogative of his class. And more, he believes it to the point where such belief becomes an effective truth. However, a trip to the lake in order to escape the fears and frustrations of his crumbling world after Paul's imprisonment teaches him that he cannot escape from himself, and that Lake Sunasquam, despite its great natural charm, is inhabited by a breed of rural Babbitt.

Although Babbitt does not love his wife Myra in the romantic fashion he reserves for the fairy girl of his dreams, he is a good husband and father. He has always provided well and liberally for his family's needs. He has financed Verona's education, as he will Ted's and Tinka's. And he has provided Myra with a comfortable home and surrounded her with all the labor-saving devices within the capabilities of his pocketbook. The difficulty is that their house is not a home, but merely a place where the family sleeps, eats, and occasionally entertains. Like a good hotel, it is impersonal in the appointments therein and in the relationships of the guests. Here the family exists in mutual respect, but with little love. This does not mean that they are incapable of love, but that natural passions and emotions which they ought to feel have been submerged by the impersonality of their surroundings, and by the dull, vapid, and standardized society of which they are a part.

It is then the inescapable dullness of Babbitt's world, inspired by standardization of almost every aspect of existence material, spiritual, and moral, which is its chief characteristic in Zenith and its environs. In fact, the whole Babbitt world is one painted in monotones; inhabited by people who think, eat, dress, talk, and live alike, people who are incapable of love, or real immorality. Only those who are outside the world of Babbittry are capable of real emotion or action. Paul Riesling is capable of love, but he never gets to experience it. The Jake Offutts and the Healy Hansens can be truly immoral because they honestly accept the fact that what they are doing is dishonest. Babbitt, like all the Babbitts of the world, is a man incapable of doing anything truly good or truly bad, but is forever doomed to inhabit the grey world between, a world filled with calculated ignorance and self-deception.

The character of Babbitt is not the only target for Lewis' **satire**. For although Babbitt provides the focal point for Lewis' **satire** in the novel, Lewis saw to it that he was mobile enough to provide a wide variety of other targets. Foremost among these targets are Prohibition (which Lewis thought an abomination) and the fuzzy reasoning which made it possible, the Social Club (in this case the Athletic Club and the Union Club), the National Guard (particularly of the Zenith variety), the Good Citizen's League (an organization representative of a wide variety of organizations ranging from various kinds of citizens' groups to the K.K.K.), evangelism, the cultural societies, and bohemianism.

As Lewis clearly demonstrated, prohibition was a law universally disregarded, valuable only because it provided Americans with a topic of conversation and a degree of pleasure because it allowed them to indulge in a universally sanctioned, if illegal, sin.

Nor did the Social Club fare much better at Lewis' hands. Within the sanctuaries of their various clubs, depending upon the members' own prominence and affluence, club members could escape the pressures of the workaday world and enjoy the good fellowship of their chosen companions as well as their dinners. In actuality, Lewis argued that membership in such clubs was merely another form of status symbol, as was revealed by the rivalry between the Athletic Club and the Union Club. The Athletic Club, however, like the vast majority of such clubs, was a failure as a status symbol except in the eyes of the members who belonged because it was neither exclusive nor athletic.

Lewis' satiric jab at the National Guard was, of course, occasioned by the fact that in the domestic confusion following World War I, the National Guard was used many times as an organization to break strikes. And as Lewis had noted, the officers' list of most guard units, like the one in Zenith, was composed primarily of members of the conservative upper-middle-class who had the most to lose if the strikes were successful. Ironically, the rank and file of these guard units was often made up of men who were acting against the very class of which they were themselves a part.

The Good Citizen's League, like many present-day extremist organizations, was to be treated by Lewis at greater length some years after *Babbitt* in *It Can't Happen Here* (1935). Its sole purpose was to persuade, through reason, intimidation, boycott, or threat, anyone who did not subscribe to or conform with its views. Not only did Lewis recognize such organizations early, but he predicted that they would operate under the guise of patriotism. Though Lewis' **satire** has not eliminated such organizations, it has made them recognizable.

Although Lewis throughout most of his adult life was not a churchgoer, he was not an irreligious man. However, his apparent attacks on religion in *Babbitt* and later in *Elmer Gantry* provoked many such accusations against him. As he had accurately recorded many other aspects of America, so he recorded some of the aspects of religion which he believed legitimate targets for his **satire**. His Reverend Drew in many respects simply represents an Americanization of the nineteenth century English vicar so common in British literature. He is modern, urbane, gentlemanly, and efficient; talented enough to be anything but a preacher. His more ebullient counterpart Mike Monday, the evangelist, probably represents Lewis' satiric portrait of the famous radio evangelist, Billy Sunday.

After World War I, Americans in greater numbers than ever before were beginning to rediscover Europe, and many of these returning pilgrims were quick to discern that the culture of their countrymen was by comparison awkward and undeveloped. Thus, in a scene which owes much to Dickens and Mark Twain, Babbitt and Myra visit a lecture of the Zenith chapter of the New Thought League, whose philosophy and teaching Lewis parodies to the point of ridicule, with the result that the lecture they hear bears a strong resemblance to the pitch of a patent medicine salesman who has become himself convinced of the efficacy of his product.

Like Babbitt, Lewis had himself escaped occasionally into the world of the bohemians only to discover that it was a world as circumscribed and limited as the world from which he was trying to escape. Tanis Judique and her friends, attempting to capture forever the fleeing shadows of their youth, pretend disdain for the conventional world. Yet, like Babbitt, most of them return to nine-to-five jobs, postponing their rebellion until their evening hours. And paradoxically and ironically, each of them yearns to be like Babbitt, a solid citizen in a financially secure world. Like most bohemians, they have chosen the guise of rebellion in order to conceal, even from themselves, their own failures. At the end of the novel, though Babbitt is still foolish, still uneducated, and will undoubtedly still make many mistakes, he is not entirely a failure.

Nor are these targets reached directly or indirectly through the person of George F. Babbitt the only targets of Lewis' **satire** in *Babbitt*. Through the medium of minor characters Lewis was able to introduce material which could otherwise not be dealt with conveniently. For example, Ted's enthusiasm for the exotic jobs to be secured through fraudulent and misleading advertising, as well as the ads which Babbitt has written himself, provide Lewis with the necessary material to explore the ethics of advertising. As "Chum" Frink, poet and advertising copywriter, later puts it, a good ad has got to have the "spill-of-speech," for the function of the advertiser is to sell products-not to proclaim truth, or to ascertain the quality, or lack of it, of the product.

And such characters as Elnora Pearl Bates, society editor for the *Advocate-Times*, and Lucille McKelvey provide Lewis with the opportunity to give the reader a fleeting and humorous glimpse of Zenith's high society with the result that they appear as merely superior Babbitts.

Although *Babbitt* is a novel without a conventional plot, what plot it does have is contained in the story of Babbitt's revolt against the **conventions** of an existence which he has lately begun to suspect as false. The fear of social censure, however, is too strong a force for him to bear. Long accustomed to his conventional and frustrating world, his revolt can only be brief and foolish. His fling with Tanis and the "bunch" and his temporary flirtation with what his friends term radicalism are doomed to ignominious failure, and he returns chastised to the fold. Only his advice to Ted at the novel's close remains of his hoped for freedom. And even then he cannot offer more than an ineffectual "do better." And such is essentially Lewis' advice to the reader.

Thus, filled with a welter of concrete detail concerning persons, places, and things, *Babbitt* appears to be a highly realistic novel whose purpose is to excoriate the stupidities of the world which it mirrors. The truth, however, is that the world of *Babbitt* has never really existed and probably never will except as the invention of Sinclair Lewis. What reality that world possesses is all on the surface. Zenith with its tall buildings, barbershops, offices, caterers, housing developments, and speakeasies, is thoroughly believable. It is solid and concrete. However, much of the data accumulated to prove the solidity of the social order of Babbitt's world has from the outset been carefully selected to reveal the dullness, the emptiness, and conditioned nature of that world.

In other words, what Lewis had done in *Babbitt* was to create a novel whose characters and situations were thoroughly under his control, a novel in which every detail was carefully chosen to prove its thesis. Thus the immature or inexperienced reader is often misled into believing that *Babbitt* is a novel which presents truth with complete objectivity. It, of course, does not, because the world of *Babbitt* is too consciously limited to be representative of reality. However, good **satire** often requires a distortion of reality. Like caricature and **parody**, which are its artistic neighbors, **satire** involves a necessary heightening in order to achieve its effects. Especially when its creator is determined to reach as large an audience as possible.

And Sinclair Lewis reached that audience. Through *Babbitt* he has convinced several generations of Americans that the way of life which they had long accepted as sacred and inviolable needed to be questioned and examined. However, the term Babbitt as it has now come to be understood bears little relation to the *Babbitt* of Lewis' novel because Lewis' *Babbitt* at least suspected that the mores of his world were false. Modern definitions regard a Babbitt as any business or professional man who adheres unquestioningly to the social and ethical standards of his group. If Lewis' *Babbitt* didn't know the answers, he at least discovered some of the questions.

Another aspect of *Babbitt* which served to increase its seeming solidity and contribute greatly to its air of reality was Lewis' uncanny knack for capturing the idiom of American speech, although, like the portraits of his characters and institutions, that speech is often heightened or carried on to unrealistic lengths. Not only are Babbitt and his friends garrulous, but they are abnormally so.

In addition, Lewis in *Babbitt* has portrayed the anti-Babbitt forces, the forces for progress of all kinds, as weak and ineffectual. Seneca Doane, the radical lawyer, though idealistic and competent, is made to appear ineffectual. Not only is the part which he plays in the novel minuscule, but whenever he is momentarily allowed to mount a real challenge to the cult of Babbittry, he is easily and resoundingly defeated. For example, when he runs for mayor against Lucas Prout, both he and the reader are aware that his cause is lost from the outset. Neither does he fare much better as one of the supporters of the Zenith general strike which appears to be broken simply because the workers are not allowed to parade.

Nor does Paul Riesling, Babbitt's alter ego, appear effective as a counter agent to the forces of Babbittry. Not only does Babbitt appear at every stage of their relationship to be the stronger and more effective of the pair, but Paul is even less prepared to carry out his personal rebellion against an unhappy marriage and a social order which he feels is destroying him. At least Babbitt's rebellion, short-lived as it is, takes the form of direct confrontation with those forces, but Paul's violent explosion reveals his inability to fight at all, except to take the kind of action which he knows can only bring about his own destruction.

Thus Lewis in *Babbitt*, as he has made the forces of Babbittry powerful, has made the forces for reform, sensitivity, and humanity weak and ineffectual. He has in each instance, of course, grossly exaggerated his case. And he has, in a sense, created the social order which he appears to record.

Always a perceptive observer of the American scene of which he was himself so much a part, Lewis caught the vulgarity, the sights, and the sounds of that scene. He never, however, lost sight of America's potential greatness. Although he could violently satirize things American, he always maintained a love and respect for the things at which he poked fun. Unfitted to be a historian, or a sociologist, Lewis chose the novel as his means of exposing the defects of American society and civilization. And he recorded clearly many aspects of that civilization for his fellow citizens to see. In his novels he has managed to portray

BRIGHT NOTES STUDY GUIDE

Americans as they believe themselves to be, and as a result, not only supplied much needed instruction, but provided his readers with the pleasures of recognition. His salesmen, boosters, butchers, bankers, bootleggers, doctors, and village idiots all ring true. As a result he achieved a rapport with a wide audience achieved by few novelists. Like Dickens and Mark Twain, Lewis attained a folksy and comradely understanding with his audience who reveled in his satiric jibes at the hypocrisies, cruelties, and vulgarities of the twentieth century existence. Lewis, however, like most satirists, was doomed in part to have most of the Babbitts among his readers peer into his mirror and see Vergil Gunch or Seneca Doane, but not themselves.

BABBITT

. . . .

Characterized early by Vernon L. Parrington as "the bad boy of American letters whose thoughts are on bent pens while the deacon is laboring in prayer," Sinclair Lewis has either excited the anger or the imagination of the literary critics. Never an effective stylist nor an especially adept literary technician, Lewis has for a third of a century defied adequate evaluation. This does not mean, however, that a host of early critics did not offer illuminating as well as interesting commentary on Lewis and his work. As for example the famous novelist and critic, James Branch Cabell, noted, "Lewis' characters are superb monsters, now and then a bit suggestive of human beings" who were by their author portrayed "with loving abhorrence."

EARLY CRITICS

Thus, as Lewis' work had critically appraised America and its mores, so his own work elicited comment in response. Among early critics of *Babbitt*, F. K. Whipple noted that the characters of *Babbitt* were "dead" and that "the dead are resolved that no one shall live," a criticism expanded by Maxwell Geismar to include the notion that *Babbitt* is a novel "set in Hell." Thus early critics noted a dichotomy between the seemingly solid nature of the reality in *Babbitt* and the artificial world which is really recorded. For *Babbitt* is not a realistic novel as some critics and readers have mistakenly believed. Like G. B. Shaw's Don Juan in Hell, *Babbitt* was Lewis' illustration that any society whose values could be measured in purely material terms was Hell; Hell because it was dull and stultifying in all its aspects. Any society whose morals, manners, clothes, cars, homes, ideas, and conversation are identical cannot be populated by human beings-only by the damned.

THE ACHIEVEMENT OF BABBITT

Although *Babbitt* was early recorded by critics as a novel which was not realistic, it was, as Alfred Kazin recorded, a novel which "had entered as completely into the national imagination as Daniel Boone." For although *Babbitt* did not record the world as it really was, it recorded the world as most Americans believed it to be. And more, it shaped the world which it purported to record, much in its own image. So much so, in fact, that the word Babbitt has entered into the American language as a synonym for all those American business or professional men who adhere to a rigid set of business or social standards.

THE SUBJECT MATTER OF BABBITT

Babbitt, however, like most of Lewis' novels, is a book based, according to Mark Schorer, on two observations: "the standardization of manners in a business culture, and the stultification of morals under middle-class convention." It becomes, then, as much a thesis novel as a **satire**, since it seeks to prove by example what it already presumes to exist, with the result that the novel is what Schorer refers to as "the method of half-truths." Nevertheless, as half-truth is better than no truth at all. To a reading public long accustomed to romantic and escapist fiction, Lewis burst like a meteor on the literary horizon. Suddenly a novelist had appeared whose function seemed to be to tear away the veils of hypocrisy from American life, a novelist who would reveal the truth long hidden behind the mythology of American middle-class righteousness. What actually happened, of course, as Alfred Kazin aptly noted, was that Lewis "confirmed Americans in the legend of their democratic humility, the suspicion that every stuffed shirt conceals a quaking heart." Thus, Americans could enjoy reading about Babbitt as long as they were certain that they were not Babbitt.

THE REALISM OF BABBITT

However, in spite of the fact that critics are generally agreed that *Babbitt* is not a truly realistic novel, it remains a very great achievement. For Lewis, with considerable skill, did successfully satirize much of what was wrong with America, even if he did not provide any workable alternatives. Moreover, nothing even remotely like *Babbitt* exists in American literature. According to Leslie Fiedler, "the journalistic thinness of Lewis is beside the point. For all of us the real facts of experience have been replaced by *Winesburg, Ohio* (Sherwood Anderson's novel) and by *Babbitt*; myth or platitude, we have invented nothing to replace them." This, of course, is a truth demonstrated by the fact that Lewis has had no legitimate successor. No one before or since has recorded the sights, sounds, language, institutions, and mores of American society so extensively or so aptly.

NOT A REPRESENTATION OF SOCIETY

Although it remains true, according to Lewis' biographer, Mark Schorer, that "what emerges [from Lewis' novels] is in fact an image and a criticism of middle-class society and not in the least a representative of it." Lewis did record that society closer to its "average" than any other American novelist. Nor is reality an absolute necessity for a satirist, for **satire** is a literary mode only rarely at home with **realism**. Heightening, exaggeration, **parody**, and caricature are its near relatives, and distortion its blood brother. For the satirist is not interested in absolute truth, but in truth sufficient to convey his meaning.

THE PURPOSE OF BABBITT

Although Lewis in *Babbitt* attacked a number of American institutions including the church, and although it is true that he probably considered himself an atheist, it remains obvious that Dorothy Thompson's comment that "God was never taken in by that" is just as true. For though Lewis treated religion somewhat cavalierly in the persons of Reverend Drew and Mike Monday, he accorded a considerable respect for Beecher Ingram, the humanitarian preacher who aided Seneca Doane. As he argued himself, he had never argued for anything or "against anything save dullness."

What then Lewis attacked in *Babbitt* as well as in other novels was complacency, the complacency which Americans in general extended to include all things American. Lewis forced America to take a hard look at itself, and according to Edward Wagenknecht, "called us back to the tradition of American independence."

LEWIS' LITERARY THESIS

This then is the actual thesis of Lewis' novels, a thesis contained in Babbitt's injunction to Ted at the novel's close, to live a freer and more independent life, to find one's own way, to think, to work, to dream for one's self and not to slavishly accept the dreams, ideas, and ways of others. *Babbitt* remains not only a novel of criticism, but of affirmation.

THE PROBLEMS OF LEWIS' STYLE

Almost every critic of Lewis had noted the deficiencies of his literary method. *Babbitt*, like most of Lewis' novels, appears a hodgepodge of episodes, connected only by the presence of George F. Babbitt. Although the method admittedly is awkward, it is effective. For it not only allowed Lewis to range widely and select material appropriate to the thesis, but according to Robert Cantwell, Lewis "thought of his writings ... in terms of the accomplishment of a foreknown task." Lewis was not so much interested in the "how" of what he wrote, but in the "what." Every novel contains its carefully conceived criticism of some aspect of the American scene. *Babbitt* explores business morality; *Elmer Gantry* explores religious hypocrisy; *It Can't Happen Here*, fascist-type organizations; and *Kingsblood Royal*, race relations. Thus Lewis was to become the recorder as well as the critic of a vast portion of the American scene, a scene which no other American novelist had surveyed so thoroughly.

BABBITT

. . . .

Question: What organizing principles did Lewis employ in the writing of *Babbitt*?

Answer: *Babbitt* is not a novel which contains a conventional plot. It is arranged instead as a series of more than thirty loosely organized episodes which achieve a kind of rough unity because most of them are concerned with the activities of a single character, George F. Babbitt. In addition, the novel achieves unity through consistency of satiric tone, and because most of the events of the novel are concerned with those aspects of American life which reveal the stultifying effects of the standardized nature of that life.

Although Lewis on occasion in *Babbitt* drew his portraits larger than life, and although in many respects Babbitt remains a caricature rather than a fully drawn character, the novel achieves its intended effect. For if Lewis was repetitive because he found middle-class life dull and repetitive, he used caricature because he believed the Babbitts of America were in reality caricatures of the human beings they might be. Thus choosing scenes selectively rather than in accordance with a strict chronology, Lewis achieved his purpose in satirizing middle-class American beliefs, practices, and morality, which were themselves the result of American education, religion, and family life.

Question: What was Sinclair Lewis' attitude toward George F. Babbitt?

Answer: Although in *Babbitt* Sinclair Lewis often violently satirized George F. Babbitt's manner of existence, he never lost his affection for Babbitt the man. Though Babbitt is obviously foolish, somewhat dishonest, ill-educated, and often dull, he is not without redeeming qualities. He is capable of unselfish friendship, as in the case of Paul; he is generally decent even though his decency is a quality largely obtained by the forces of conventions; and he is loyal though his loyalties are often misguided and misdirected.

In addition, Lewis, like most of us, was attracted to Babbitt's faults because he shared them. Born and bred in a small Midwestern town, Lewis never quite lost the provincial air which his Midwestern twang proclaimed, nor did he ever quite lose his affection for the peculiarly American qualities of boisterous good fellowship (Lewis could on occasion be a charming host or guest). And finally, Lewis could not entirely condemn Babbitt's grasping after money because he was himself to write potboilers to capitalize on his fame as the author of *Main Street* and *Babbitt*.

And further, although Lewis informs the reader that Babbitt was a joiner primarily because it was good for business, the reader is not unaware that Babbitt is equally activated by motives of a more unselfish nature. Babbitt is convinced that the public service which he performs in the campaign of Lucas Prout, or on the Sunday School Advisory Committee, serves ends beyond his personal gain. Indeed, Babbitt's eternal wondering if what he is doing is right is a sign that his intentions are more extensive than those he admits to, and a sign of his essential decency.

Question: What are some of the major targets for Sinclair Lewis' **satire** in *Babbitt*?

Answer: The primary target for Sinclair Lewis' **satire** in *Babbitt* is the effect of standardization on the manners and morals of middle-class American society. Babbitt's world is bounded on all sides by institutions and customs whose sole function appears to be to channel his life and activities in prescribed directions.

He is forced, if he wishes to be successful, to accept the dubious morality of the business world of which he is a part; he is forced, if he wishes to gain acceptance and approval of his friends and neighbors, to subscribe to the codes of conduct which his position as a member of respectable society demands; and finally, he is forced to engage in a variety of pseudosocial, business, and political activities expected of a man of some prominence.

Lewis' primary target is, of course, reached through a number of more specific secondary ones including the school, the church, the lodge, the club, and a vast variety of business connected organizations. The school is satirized through the medium of Babbitt, Ted, and Verona, who are its products; the church in the person of the businesslike and spiritually ineffectual Reverend John Drew; the lodge, the Boosters, the **convention,** and the club through a host of lesser characters.

Even such a purely social activity as a dinner for friends is made to serve the ends of Lewis' **satire**. For example, the dinner which the Babbitts hold for their neighbors and friends in the early part of the novel contains Lewis' satiric comment on the standardization of dress, conversation, manners, and fare which were the unvarying ingredients of such affairs.

Thus Lewis in *Babbitt* satirized virtually every aspect of middle-class American existence in the nineteen twenties. However, it must be noted that Lewis' presentation of that society is a one-sided view. Like all good satirists, he did not admit to any awareness that the portrait he was painting was in any way incomplete. Actually, though the novel is filled with varying kinds and degrees of Babbitts, one feels certain that the world was not, not even the world of Zenith.

Question: Why did Lewis feel it necessary to create Zenith? What advantages are the result of that creation?

Answer: Because he was writing a novel which dealt with contemporary America, Lewis felt constrained to invent places as well as people since by doing so he could write more freely. Indeed, for *Babbitt*, as well as *Arrowsmith* and *Dodsworth* which followed in the Zenith trilogy, Lewis invented not only a neighborhood or a small town, but a whole state which he then proceeded to geographically detail and populate so that those who have read all three novels feel as much at home in Zenith and its environs as they do in their own states and towns.

In *Babbitt* not only does the reader observe Babbitt as he talks, argues, or does business with other characters, but the reader observes him getting a manicure at the Pompian barbershop, buying bootleg liquor from Healy Hansen's saloon, selling cemetery lots for Linden Lane, and buying ice cream at the Maison Veechis, Zenith's leading catering establishment. The result is that the careful reader knows when Babbitt travels north, east, south or west, where he is likely to be going and what he is likely to see.

And finally part of Lewis' intended **satire** is achieved through places and institutions rather than through people. For these concrete objects are the symbols which helped him to reveal the underlying maladies of a society which Lewis believed sick. What Lewis was attacking were those elements of standardization and corruption which stultify and destroy individuals. After all, what difference did it really make whether one lived in Glen Oriole or Avon Lea, or was buried in Linden Lane or Wildwood Cemetery.

Question: What relevance does *Babbitt* have for modern Americans?

Answer: Although *Babbitt* is a novel which specifically deals with America of the nineteen twenties, it is essentially a novel which satirizes universal and eternal human foibles and follies. And in many respects, George F. Babbitt represents a kind of provincial American Everyman, for his social climbing, his fawning respect for wealth, and his hypochondria are traits common to a large segment of the humanity of any age.

In addition, many of the American institutions and customs toward which Lewis directed his most biting **satire** still exist, for many Americans are still absorbed by boosterism, prejudice, and status symbols, all of which have simply assumed more sophisticated guises. Whole segments of our society are still absorbed by deceptive advertising and high-pressure salesmanship. A gap still exists between what Americans say and what they believe. America is still plagued by the Klan and the Good Citizen's League. Political chicanery is yet a too common feature of our political system. And the arguments which divide the business, professional, and labor segments of our society have not all been resolved.

Thus, although much of *Babbitt* appears dated because the language of many of its characters is now obsolete, and because it appears to record the foibles of an ageless sophisticated than our own, it actually records and satirizes the common failings of humanity, and points an accusing finger at the dangers of a mechanized and standardized society whose values can only be measured in material terms.

Question: What are some of the techniques by which Lewis creates character?

Answer: Lewis created his characters in many ways. The first key to a character's personality may be noted in the way in which he is described. For example, Babbitt's suits are gray or brown, conservatively cut, his shoes are standard, his family typical, and from his watch chain his Elk's tooth dangles, and Healy Hansen, the local bootlegger, is dressed in a tan silk shirt, a checkered vest and burning brown trousers. Second characters are revealed through their peculiar manner of speech. As Babbitt and most of the Zenith Boosters are revealed by their boisterous and often raucous speech, Paul Riesling is revealed by his quiet manner, Myra by her deferential manner, and Vergil Gunch by his patronizing one. And each is further revealed by the degree to which his speech reveals the success, failure, or lack of education. Third, characters are revealed by the place which they inhabit. The standardized homes of Floral Heights can only be inhabited by standardized and conventional human beings. Of course, almost all of the characters of *Babbitt* are standardized men.

In addition, Lewis employed the more usual means of creating character. Speaking in his own person as narrator he tells us what characters are like, he tells us what activities they undertake, and by the manner in which he tells us, we approve or disapprove. For example, when Babbitt fires Stanley Graff for dishonesty, not only is the reader conscious that Babbitt has just realized a substantial profit from the Traction Company deal, but he is told that for some time Babbitt had suspected that Graff was being dishonest. And finally, Lewis as omniscient author comments in his own person ironically or satirically on his characters' thoughts and actions, words and deeds, and reveals through an **irony** sometimes subtle, sometimes bludgeoning, the dichotomy which exists between them.

Question: What solution, if any, does Lewis propose to the dilemmas of standardized existence?

Answer: Although Lewis in general was angered by the consequences of standardization, he was not unaware of the benefits which might accrue from mass production. What he objected most strenuously to in *Babbitt* was mass-produced man. However, at no point in the novel did Lewis point to some specific means by which humans could escape the inevitable stultifying effects of a culture whose art, education, and thought was mass produced. Not even the radical lawyer, Seneca Doane, is certain that mass production is not more a blessing than a curse. Thus in *Babbitt*, Lewis appears unable to propose any solutions to the way of life which is the inevitable result of such standardization because he was unable to propose any workable substitute for procuring the necessities for existence for a mass society. Indeed, the only positive advice which he was able to offer at all was the advice at the novel's end which Babbitt offered to Ted, to live his life as he thinks best. This of course is not a solution since Ted, like Babbitt, is unlikely to be strong enough to resist the pressures toward conformity which will be exerted on him from many quarters in the future.

The only other solutions, then, which Lewis proposed were the obvious and hardly original notions that man must face life honestly and courageously. However, it is the legitimate function of the satirist to point out failings and not to propose solutions, for those who propose dogmatic solutions are not satirists but propagandists or theorists. Moreover, Lewis was undoubtedly aware that there were no easy solutions to the dilemmas of the twentieth century which he exposed to view, and he was undoubtedly even more aware that the beginning of any solution begins with the recognition that a problem exists. What *Babbitt* accomplished was to make Americans acutely aware that new problems of **convention** and conformity as a by-product of standardization did and do exist.

BIBLIOGRAPHY AND GUIDE TO RESEARCH

Any research paper should be based on reliable texts. Although there is no definitive edition of Sinclair Lewis' works, his novels are currently available in a wide variety of inexpensive paperback editions.

There are innumerable biographical and critical books and articles on Sinclair Lewis and his work. The following is an annotated list, arranged alphabetically by suggested research topics. However, since Sinclair Lewis was a comparatively recent novelist, his contributions to the novel and true extent of his value as a social critic have yet to be definitively evaluated.

BIOGRAPHIES OF SINCLAIR LEWIS

Questions to consider: How much of Sinclair Lewis' life appears in his literature? In *Babbitt* in particular? What attitudes did Lewis have toward his own work?

Grebstein, Sheldon N. *Sinclair Lewis.* New York: 1962.

Lewis, Grace Hegger. *With Love from Gracie*. New York: 1955. Readable, reveals many aspects of Lewis' personality unrecorded by other biographers.

Sheean, Vincent. *Dorothy and Red*. Boston: 1963. A very personal biography of Lewis' relationship with Dorothy Thompson, his second wife.

Schorer, Mark. *Sinclair Lewis: An American Life*. New York: 1961. The standard biography, extensive, scholarly, readable.

Van Doren, Carl. *Sinclair Lewis: A Biographical Sketch*. New York: 1933. An older biography but still contains good bibliography of early articles and books.

Wolfe, S. J. *Drawn from Life*. Whittlesey House: 1932.

THE BACKGROUND OF BABBITT

Questions to consider: How nearly does *Babbitt* record the actual **conventions** of the society which it portrays? How accurate is Lewis' recreation of the actual speech and appearance of the characters in *Babbitt*? How effective is Sinclair Lewis' **satire** in *Babbitt*? What are some of the institutions singled out for Lewis' **satire** in *Babbitt*? What contributions did Lewis make to American critical thought?

Commager, Henry Steele. *The American Mind*. New Haven: 1950. Deals with changing American thought and the influence of Lewis and others on that thought.

Canby, Henry Seidel. "Fiction Sums up a Century," in R. E. Spiller, et al. *Literary History of the United States*. (New York: 1955) Chap. 72.

Cantwell, Robert. *After the Genteel Tradition.* ed. Malcolm Cowley. New York: 1937.

Gaus, Christian. "Sinclair Lewis vs. his Education," *Saturday Evening Post*, CCIV (December 26, 1931). Explores Lewis' anti-intellectual attitude.

Geismar, Maxwell. *The Last of the Provincials: The American Novel, 1915-1925.* Boston: 1947. One of the best critical evaluations of Lewis' work.

Hicks, Granville. "Sinclair Lewis and the Good Life," *English Journal, College Edition*, XXV (1936). Concerned with value of Lewis as a social critic.

Horton, Rod W. and Edwards, H. W. "The Twenties," *Backgrounds of American Literary Thought.* New York: 1952, pp. 292-330. Excellent background material for the student who wishes to understand the attitudes current in the 1920s.

Horton, Thomas D. "Sinclair Lewis: The Symbol of an Era," *North American Review*, CCXLVII (1940), 474-493. A brief evaluation of Lewis' position as a novelist.

McNally, W. J. "Mr. Babbitt, Meet Sinclair Lewis," *Nation* CXXV (1927). Explores Sinclair Lewis' sympathies for *Babbitt.*

Parrington, Vernon L. *Main Currents in American Thought* (vol. 3) New York: 1927-1930. An excellent three-volume study of American literary directions. Volume three deals with Lewis and the twentieth century.

Lewis, Sinclair. "Self Conscious America," *American Mercury*, VI (1925), 199-239. Lewis' own explanation of his work and its critics.

Schorer, Mark. "Sinclair Lewis and the Method of Half Truth," *Modern American Fiction*, New York: Oxford, 1963, pp. 95-111. Good evaluation of Lewis' method in *Babbitt* and especially in *Elmer Gantry.*

Schorer, Mark (ed.). *Sinclair Lewis: A Collection of Critical Essays*. Englewood-Cliffs, N.J.: 1962. An excellent collection of essays by a number of gifted Lewis critics including Robert Cantwell, Joseph Wood Krutch, Lewis Mumford, and Edmund Wilson.

Stallman, R. W. "Sinclair Lewis as a Teacher," *New York Times Book Review*, October 22, 1961.

SINCLAIR LEWIS AS A LITERARY ARTIST

Questions to consider: How does Sinclair Lewis rank as a literary stylist? What techniques did Lewis employ in the creation of his novels? To what authors is Lewis indebted for some aspects of his technique?

Auchincloss, Louis. "Master Journalist of American Fiction," *Harpers Magazine*, November 1961, pp. 124 ff.

Beck, Warren. "How Good is Sinclair Lewis?" *College English*, IX (1948), 173–180.

Johnson, G. W. "Romance and Mr. Babbitt," *NR* CXXIV, (January 29, 1951) 14–15. An exploration of Babbitt's daydreams.

Morris, Floyd. "Sinclair Lewis, His Critics and the Public," *North American Review* CCXLV (1938), 381–390.

Sherman, Stuart. *The Significance of Sinclair Lewis*. New York: Harcourt Brace, 1922.

Smith, Harrison (ed.). *From Maine Street to Stockholm: Letters of Sinclair Lewis*. New York: Harcourt Brace, 1952.

Van Doren, Carl. "Sinclair Lewis and Sherwood Anderson," *Century Magazine* CX (1925), 362–369. A good evaluation of Lewis as a novelist of the twenties.

BOOKS WHICH DEAL GENERALLY WITH LEWIS AND HIS WORK

Questions to consider: Evaluate Sinclair Lewis as an American novelist of the twentieth century. What do critics generally believe to be Lewis' best work? Why?

Heiney, Donald. *Recent American Fiction.* New York: Barrons, 1961. A good survey of modern American writing.

Kazin, Alfred. *On Native Grounds.* New York: Harcourt, Brace & World, Inc., Reprinted by Doubleday, 1956. (Anchor Paperback). A survey and a critical commentary on the American novel since 1890.

Wagenknecht, Edward. *Cavalcade of the American Novel.* New York: Holt, Rinehart and Winston, 1964. Good general survey of American fiction, contains good bibliography.

BIBLIOGRAPHIC GUIDES

The following is a list of bibliographic material to aid the serious student who wishes a more comprehensive list of material on Sinclair Lewis and his work.

"Annual Bibliography," *PMLA* (1922 -).

"Articles on *American Literature* appearing in current periodicals (1929 -)," Quarterly in *American Literature*.

[Johnson, Thomas H. Ed.]. Volume III of *Spiller. Literary History of the United States*. Supplement ed. Richard M. Ludwig. New York: 1959.

Leary, Lewis. *Articles on American Literature*, 1900–1950. Durham, N.C.: 1954.

Safavieh

CPSIA information can be obtained
at www.ICGtesting.com
Printed in the USA
LVHW082150100622
720994LV00015B/1500